Three Pagodas Pass

ALSO BY GEORGE FETHERLING

One Russia, Two Chinas
Running Away to Sea: Round the World on a Tramp Freighter
Travels by Night: A Memoir of the Sixties
Selected Poems
Madagascar: Poems & Translations

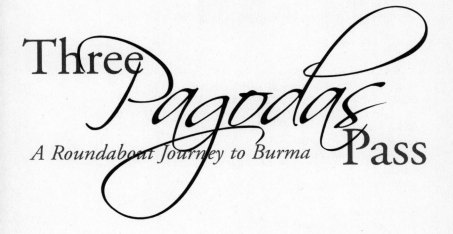

Three Pagodas Pass

A Roundabout Journey to Burma

GEORGE FETHERLING

SUBWAY
VANCOUVER

Copyright © 2002 by George Fetherling
Printed and bound in Canada

ISBN 0-9687163-2-6
National Library of Canada Cataloguing in Publication Data

Fetherling, George
  Three Pagodas Pass: a roundabout journey to Burma/George Fetherling.

  ISBN 0-9687163-2-6

  1. Fetherling, George—Journeys—Burma. 2. Burma—Description
and travel. I. Title.
DS527.7.F47 2002   959.105221   C2002-911130-7

Subway Books Ltd.
1819 Pendrell Street, Unit 203
Vancouver, B.C. V6G 1T3
Canada
E-mail: *subway@interlog.com*

Editor: Michael Carroll
Design and Production: Jen Hamilton

Canadian orders:
Customer Order Department
University of Toronto Press
5201 Dufferin Street
Toronto, Ontario M3H 5T8
Canada

US orders:
University of Toronto Press
2250 Military Road
Tonawanda, New York 14150
Tel.: (716) 693-2768
Fax: (716) 692-7479

Toll-free ordering from Canada or the US:
Tel.: 1-800-565-9523
Fax: 1-800-221-9985
E-mail: *utpbooks@utpress.utoronto.ca*

For Keith and Mary Maillard

CONTENTS

RANGOON
VIA CASABLANCA

*E*arlier that day Athens had been torn apart by riots. The city of narrow streets and fascinating graffiti was turning septic. What started it all was President Bill Clinton's arrival. A pair of identical planes called Air Force One dominated the runway. The American chief executive always travels with two so that terrorists won't know which is real and which the decoy. Greek special forces and US snipers on the terminal roof covered both equally; they weren't going to give away the game (two-card monte).

Immigration was perfunctory and Customs had shut down completely, except for an old grey cat sleeping atop a disconnected metal detector. The authorities wanted to clear the area as soon as possible. We were herded into coaches for the short trip to the docks at Piraeus. Most major streets were closed for security reasons. Central Athens seemed bereft of people except for cops on every corner, small clusters of them, wearing fluorescent green rain ponchos: the same shade of green you see on certain houseflies in the summer. The port area was deserted too. We drove under a long line of protruding sterns, reading the Greek names on each freighter. Our own vessel lay tied up at the end, illuminated by what looked like Christmas lights. Bernadette and I had been seeing each other for a while, and we would be sharing a small cabin in this old hulk as an experiment to see if we could get along well enough during two months at sea to coexist on land. We would know the answer by the time we reached French Polynesia. There we would both leave the ship, she to return to her job in Vancouver, I to continue on alone to Burma, where the civil war, already in its baroque period, was about to enter its fifty-first consecutive year. At the beginning as at the end, and at most every point in between, I ran into a wall of politics.

During the seagoing portion of the journey, we were merely hitching a ride on what was being marketed as a round-the-world adventure for travellers with scientific and ethnological interests. This was the ship's maiden voyage under its latest identity, but it had had a long and colourful career. If the vessel had been in show business it would have been Elizabeth Taylor. It was built in 1944 in New Jersey as a troop carrier. One of our fellow passengers realized midway through the trip that he had gone to Europe aboard it as a soldier in 1945. At various times it had been the SS *President Roosevelt* of the American Presidents Line and the SS Something Else of the Dollar Line. Some pieces of bedding still had *Emerald Seas* or other obsolete names stitched on them.

The ship had plied the Atlantic and the Pacific as a liner and the Miami-to-Nassau run as a cruise vessel. Most recently it had done two years as a floating dormitory in Lisbon. The company that had leased it for what undoubtedly will be the last ten years of its life had advertised that the ship was completely overhauled, refitted, and redecorated for this voyage. In fact, some difficulty between the lessee and the Greek owners—an accounting snafu involving payments allegedly due at certain times—had left much of the work unfinished. Some passengers complained of sewage backing up in their cabins, others of ceilings collapsing on the bunks. Brochures promised elegant accommodation, computer classrooms, resident experts on every-thing from ecology to Renaissance art, with passengers free to draw on a high-tech communications centre and a specialized library of two thousand volumes. A yuppie paradise at sea. No one should ever believe advertising brochures, but many of the naive passengers did and, as a result, were in a state of litigious agitation about the gap between hype and reality. As for Bernadette and me, we were determined to sit back and enjoy it all. After all, we were simply stowaways of a sort, travelling for free.

Unlike many other passengers, who had cabins that—like Athens—looked as though they hadn't been redecorated since the 1960s or maybe even the 1950s, Bernadette and I had a little hooch aft on the lowermost deck, closest to the keel, that had more the feel of the 1940s when showers were called shower-baths and Princess Margaret was Princess Margaret Rose. Many a bobbysoxer must have adjusted herself in the bathroom mirror before heading up top to jitterbug, I thought. In short, this was a shakedown cruise on which everything shook down or fell down. There was no Internet communication worthy of the name: satellite problems. For a while there were no working computers at all except on the bridge. The library consisted only of a couple of hundred travel guides and thrillers, many of them duplicate copies, under heavy security lest they be stolen by the card players who monopolized the room. We had three different pursers in the time we were aboard. The first disappeared mysteriously to be replaced by another who was dismissed for cause after slugging his superior, only to be supplanted by a Greek whose sole word of English was *yes*, uttered with absolute conviction. "May I cash a traveller's cheque?" *Yes*. But there was no money in the till. "I've foolishly locked myself out of my cabin. Can you let me in, please?" *Yes*. But there was no spare key.

The most expensive quarters were on Diamond Deck, and the other levels likewise bore the names of gemstones. Bernadette and I began referring to ours as Zircon. When we first boarded, we were met and had our hands individually shaken by the chairman of the company. Bernadette noticed we were, with one or two exceptions, the youngest adults: hardly yuppies but only, by default, the most nearly yuppie-like persons to be seen. "Their strategy has obviously failed," said Bernadette. "They couldn't get the yups, because they're in their peak earning years. They can afford the tickets but not the four months off to go round the world. So at the last minute the company's gone after big blocs of seniors, discounting like mad to fill the space." I wasn't sure such people would find the appointments, being more of their own era, as charming as we did. The chairman wore a weak, weary smile. "I bet he's not coming along with us," Bernadette said (she was right). "My guess is he's leaving tonight with Clinton on one of the Air Force Ones."

His loss, I thought. The antediluvian hull strained a bit as we got under way after dinner when everyone was already in bed. The ship was under orders for Tunis and Casablanca and then out into the Atlantic, with calls at the Canary Islands, Cape Verde, Salvador da Bahia, Rio de Janiero, Buenos Aires, the Falklands, Antarctica, Tierra del Fuego, Valparaíso, Easter Island, Pitcairn Island, Papeete, and so on, back to the Mediterranean. The next morning, our first day at sea, when there was no turning back, Bernadette announced she had deliberately left without her antidepressants, intending to go cold turkey as part of the experiment in which the two of us were engaged. When she said this, I scrambled up two flights of stairs to the water line and looked desperately for land on the horizon. There was none. Well, what with this free passage (for I was writing some newspaper travel pieces), combined with enough frequent-flyer points to take me from Tahiti to Bangkok, I'd at least be getting to Burma for a month the only way I could afford. I would arrive there as the poppy harvest was still in progress but before the monsoon returned.

Why in God's name did I want to go to Burma, especially when to do so is to risk opprobrium at home? Let me try to explain. Bounded by China on the north, Thailand on the east, and India and Bangladesh on the west, Burma once had one of the most robust economies in Southeast Asia. Although small, it was the world's leading exporter of rice, and was rich in precious gems and exportable hardwoods. It is now one of the neediest nations on Earth, with a per capita income of US$200 a year, according to some sources. This figure puts it on a par with the poorest parts of Africa. Even in Nepal, a place prosperity has eluded, the equivalent figure is US$379. What's more, under British rule, which lasted from the early nineteenth century to just after the Second World War, Burma was as free as European colonialism permitted, with a vigorous and unfettered press and an elected assembly. For the past two generations, however, it has been ruled by a military dictatorship that is nominally communist but largely concerned with making money through drug trafficking.

In recent years the Taliban in Afghanistan, one of the few regimes even harsher and more frightening, had cut into Burma's reliance on heroin. So had the rise of methamphetamines (*yaa baa*—the words used in both Thailand and Burma) and ecstasy (*yaa ee*). But that hadn't kept Burma from continuing to occupy as important a place in the heroin trade as South Africa continues to hold in the diamond business, despite the new mines in Canada and elsewhere. Burma is a terrifying example of the present state of world affairs in the post–cold war era, because it combines the worst features of the excesses of communism and the excesses of the marketplace.

The country is under martial law. Citizens who speak out against the junta, or might do so, are routinely imprisoned and tortured. Tens of thousands of Burmese are taken into indentured servitude to work on government building projects. Admittedly there is a fine line between corvée and slavery. What's practised in Burma involves chains and is known by the old Asian euphemism *porterage*. Some civilians are used as human land-mine detectors. At the same time the government wages a war of extermination against the other distinct cultures known as the hill tribes, all the while using the lure of the hill tribes' diverse customs and languages to entice adventure tourists from the West with their badly needed hard currency.

The junta long operated under the name the State Law and Order Restoration Council. More recently it had a US public-relations firm create a more sympathetic-sounding name: the State Peace and Development Council. Whether called SLORC or SPDC, the junta insists—demands—that the country be called Myanmar, stating this was what it was named before the Anglo-Burmese Wars. In fact, there was no country as such until the British arrived and unified a strange collection of warring fiefdoms into the Union of Burma. Burmese have little choice but to follow this dictate. Outsiders are under no such compulsion, and the name they use reflects their politics. People who say Myanmar (and Yangon for its capital) thus instantly identify themselves with the thugs who run this physically beautiful country as a private preserve. Persons interested in human rights say Burma (and Rangoon). Most western newspapers call it Myanmar, tacitly expressing their support for the generals or at least revealing their ignorance of what's going on in the country. The Myanmar-users are often aligned to western business interests that enrich the Burmese leadership and military. Burma-users tend to support economic sanctions against the country and for the most part refuse to set foot in Burma lest they put into the junta's hands money they know will never filter down to the ordinary people.

Such being the case, and in view of my support for the latter camp, why was I so eager to go there that I made a long, drawn-out journey more than halfway round the world on the cheap? Perhaps I wanted to see for myself how bad the situation really is. Very little accurate news about Burma reaches the outside world except through the free press in Bangkok and the enterprise of the *Far Eastern Economic Review*, and very little of what does reach the West appears in the western media. Ever less news about the outside world penetrates Burma, owing to tight censorship and rigid control over all forms of electronic communication. Western activists and their supporters stay in touch with developments through electronic newsgroups. A montage of headlines from one of these gives the flavour.

Release of Political Prisoners Key to Future of Talks
Refugees Granted Asylum in Guam Despite HIV Status
Naga Villagers Seek Refuge in India
Thousands Caught Up in Thai Border Crackdown
Condition of Elderly Political Prisoners Deteriorates
International Labour Organization Won't Let Junta Off the Hook on Forced Labour
Amnesty, Human Rights Watch: Forced Labour Persists in Myanmar
Junta Signs Up with Kremlin for Surplus MIG-29s
The Strange Case of the Disappearing Speed Pills
Na-Sa-Ka Blamed for Attacks on Mosques in Maungdaw
Relief Team Reaches Nagas Burned Out of Their Homes
Canadian Imports from Burma on Steep Upward Curve
Dengue Fever Epidemic Hits Mawlamyaing Area
World Health Organisation Rep Deplores Lack of Funds for HIV/AIDS Campaign
Junta in Negotiations to Buy Russian Nuclear Reactor
News from One of the Worst Hell-Holes on Earth
Myanmar Authorities Probing Deadly Bomb Attack
Junta Speechmaker Takes a Hard Line on Forced Labour
Student Activist Dies Following Eleven Years in Prison
Myanmar Migrants Fail in Search for Foreign Haven
Another Political Prisoner Dies in Burma's Jails
Burma Called "Largest Prison for Journalists in Asia"
Canadian Athletes Entertain Prisons Minister.

In the above list "Myanmar" is, of course, being used ironically, sarcastically.

In any case, the necessity of my somehow getting to Burma to write about it was underscored when one of Canada's most senior commentators on world affairs confessed in conversation he really didn't know anything about the place beyond the little everybody else knew. To wit, that it is ruled by generals who have changed its name. With coaching he remembered that an election was held in the 1980s [in 1990, I interrupted, after the spontaneous uprising in 1988] and the woman democrat with the strange name [Aung San Suu Kyi, I chipped in] was elected, only to be prevented from taking office [being under house arrest for long periods]. "Didn't she win the Nobel Peace Prize?" he asked.

"Yes," I replied. "In 1991, putting her in the august company of Henry Kissinger."

He knew nothing about the resistance, telling me he guessed that the Palestine Liberation Organisation represented probably the longest ongoing insurgency in the world today. In fact, the Palestinian record is tied with that of the Burmese hill tribes, some of whom began fighting the central government in 1948 and are still at it. My kind of people.

Once upon a time one of the most tenacious of these minorities, the Karen, were fighting in the suburbs of Rangoon. Now they're confined to a few ever-shrinking patches of jungle along the border with Thailand. There the Burmese government (made up of Burmans, which is an ethnological distinction—unlike Burmese, which is a purely political one) has been trying to eradicate them for years. Each dry season brings a new offensive against these fascinating cultural groups, or the few who haven't long since been co-opted or beaten into submission. Lately there have been spotty signs of new resistance along the Indian border by the Chin, a group so little known that the last important English-language book on them was published in 1896, as well as by the Wa on the other side of the country (though some Wa have joined with the junta to fight the Shan). These, like others, including at least some of the much-splintered and factionalized Karen, have themselves had to turn to drug trafficking (chemical drugs mostly) in order to buy provisions and matériel.

The struggle has a religious complexion that is both obvious and profound. The junta and the Tatmadaw, its huge army, are nominally Buddhist, though in view of their actions one might question the depth of their belief as it relates to nonviolence. Burmans in general are deeply observant Buddhists, as are all but a minority of the hill tribes. One cannot help but wonder whether the hill tribes' higher level of devotion hasn't prevented them from making a stronger show of armed resistance. In this connection it's interesting to note that the Karen subgroup that has been fighting the longest is the one that was converted to Christianity by British missionaries. Give a Baptist a gun and one faces a fierce opponent untroubled by prohibitions against violence. Atop this mess sits the charismatic but also enigmatic figure of Daw Aung San Suu Kyi.

She is the refined-looking, British-educated daughter of Bogyke [General] Aung San (aka Bo Teza), the father of the Burmese independence movement who, along with seven others, was gunned down in the executive council room of the Secretariat in Rangoon in 1948, the year after his daughter's birth. The shootings, which took place virtually on the eve of Burma's independence from Britain, have perpetuated the instability and repression that have characterized the country ever since. U Saw, the former prime minister, was hanged for masterminding the murders, but suspicion has always lingered that the orders came from Ne Win, who is still alive aged about ninety, the father of the present junta. In 2002 some of Ne Win's family were arrested after an attempted countercoup that he is thought to have been behind.

Burmese politics is the most complicated subject I know that doesn't actually involve math, but here is a rough summary of some modern events.

In August 1940, fifteen months after Britain sent out Sir Reginald Dorman-Smith to be governor general of Burma, Aung San went underground as one of the legendary Thirty Comrades and began training in the arts of insurgency for use against the British. Ne Win was another of the Thirty. A week after their attack on Pearl Harbor the Japanese entered Thailand and Burma. Both the Thais and the Burmese chose to cooperate with the Japanese—in the latter case, only after severe Japanese bombing raids brought some of the most influential citizens into line. Aung San saw a Burma dominated by the Japanese as preferable to one dominated by the British, and became a major general commanding the Japanese-backed Burmese Defence Force (later called the Burmese Independence Army, the Burma National Army, and the Patriotic Burmese Forces), a job for which he was later invested with the Order of the Rising Sun by Emperor Hirohito. With his help, or at least his noninterference, the Japanese continued their conquest of Burma, which they planned to use as a stepping stone to India. By June 1942, Aung San was warning his men "not to interfere in the administration of the country [and] to keep out of party politics."

In 1943 Ne Win replaced Aung San as commander. In August 1944, with the outcome of the war becoming clear, Aung San turned against the Japanese. In October the British takeback of Burma began in earnest, and six months later Aung San helped the British effort by leading a revolt against the Japanese. The following month the Japanese withdrew from Rangoon for good. In March 1946, with the war over, Dorman-Smith considered having Aung San arrested for allegedly killing a village headman for being a British sympathizer early in the war. This threat may have helped convince Aung San that Burma should reject membership in the Commonwealth when it finally became independent. On June 19, 1947, the Constituent Assembly declared for a republic. On the morning of June 19 a team of gunmen barged into the cabinet room and shot Aung San and the others. Aung San was struck by thirteen bullets, his brother by eight.

U Saw, a former far-right newspaper publisher who had been

interned by the British in Uganda for the duration of the war after serving as Burma's prime minister from September 1940 to January 1942, was tried for masterminding the murders. In May 1948 he was executed in Insein Prison, later notorious as a place of torture by the regime of Ne Win, who led a military coup in 1962, thus establishing the present system of government. Also executed were the three actual triggermen. On January 4, 1948, the Republic of Burma was inaugurated.

Others killed in the attack were various ethnic, religious, and political leaders; for in addition to negotiating independence from Britain, Aung San had brokered peace between and among most of Burma's ethnic groups: a set of accords that, sadly, died with him, a fact that has shaped Burmese politics in subsequent years. The room in which the killings took place is now a Buddhist meditation centre.

In 1988 Ne Win was superseded but perhaps not entirely displaced by the present junta, and there was a nationwide revolt, which was cruelly and violently suppressed. Suu Kyi of the coalition called the National League for Democracy agitated for a return to multiparty elections such as had been held during the last decades of British rule. The western Left tends to idealize her as someone like themselves. In fact, she is at the conservative end of the liberal spectrum, favouring the restoration of human and civil rights, certainly, but also western investment to help rebuild the economy. With more violence in the air, the junta acceded to the call for an election and rigged it in its favour to an extent that would have made old-time Chicago politicians blush. Despite this, the voters awarded three hundred and ninety-two of the four hundred and eighty-five contested seats to the NLD, whereupon the junta simply abrogated the results, putting Suu Kyi under house arrest (not for the last time) and imprisoning many of the successful candidates. From this period dates her form of passive resistance based on Gandhian principles.

In the West the last time such a series of events took place—a right-wing dictatorship calling an election, losing, and then nullifying the outcome—the result was the Spanish Civil War of the 1930s when people from many other western nations, including Canada, came to the aid of the legitimate democratic government. Why hasn't something similar happened with regard to Burma? The answers, I believe, are two.

The first is that everyone is afraid of offending the United States, which is afraid of offending the People's Republic of China, the only neighbour with which Burma gets along and its only powerful friend in the world community, the state that has rebuilt and rearmed its land forces and navy and built it an enormous base in Burmese territory in the Andaman Islands off India. There is a body of experts, with whom, I should point out, I disagree, holding that China's periodic threats against Taiwan are a feint to distract attention from its ambitions in the Indian Ocean, that like the Japanese before them their eye is on the subcontinent. I don't doubt China feels it has strategic interests in the Indian Ocean, but I see no reason why the Indian Ocean and Taiwan should be mutually exclusive issues. In any case, this is the China after which the United States still slavers as a market for its goods and services but whose government it fears. No matter what Washington says, there are still two superpowers in the world, albeit very different ones, and China is the other. It's axiomatic (for years now the information has been appearing even in *Newsweek*) that the US intelligence community, in its unceasing computer war-gaming, has been trying to create a scenario in which the United States would win a war against China, but so far hasn't come up with one. Read this into the fact that the United States removed Burma from its list of drug-trading states, preferring to continue concentrating on Latin America, which is comparatively small potatoes but doesn't have China as an ally.

The second reason for western ignorance about Burma is that Suu Kyi refuses to leave her country and take up a position in exile that would permit her to spread the word through the media skills she possesses in such abundance. One does well in this respect to compare Burma with Tibet. The latter has the exiled Dalai Lama to serve as a magnet for attention. As a result, Tibet has become the favourite cause of Hollywood celebrities and through them is known to all, while few are aware of the worse situation in Burma. This is not to disregard the way the PRC has tried to dismantle Tibetan culture. It's only to point out that Burma may be the loser for Suu Kyi's hard-line passive resistance: passive aggression as the Freudian generations might have called it. Mine is a view, I confess, that isn't popular among western Burmophiles, who favour economic retaliation and Gandhianism as the way to bring the junta to its knees. This despite the lesson of history that Gandhianism, for the most part, works only against the British or at least the semi-British such as the former South African regime. In my view, Burma doesn't need a Gandhi (suitable for driving out a foreign power); it needs a T. E. Lawrence (to unify the tribes).

For fear of not being able to return, Suu Kyi refused to leave Burma even when her British husband, Michael Aris, lay dying of cancer in the United Kingdom. Aris, ironically, was a crusader for the cause of Tibet. In addition to the undoubted personal agonies that decision imposed, it also meant the oppressed and terrorized of Burma have no one to speak for them on *Larry King Live*. In today's world that is the same as being ignored.

All of this points up the ethical dilemma of anyone like me going to Burma period. The Lonely Planet guidebooks, published by an Australian company, are the Baedekers of the baby-boom generation, carried, it sometimes seems, by every English-speaking or European trekker or adventure traveller going to any country in the developing world. There was thus an international outcry when the book known as *Lonely Planet Burma* when it first appeared in 1979 became *Lonely Planet Myanmar* in the seventh revised and expanded edition in January 2000. The change came despite the fact that many of those who otherwise would seem to be the book's natural audience refuse to travel in Burma on principle, feeling that whatever money they spend, even for visa fees, only supports the dictatorship. Until the Asian monetary crisis of 1997, by the way, such visas were valid for a week; now visas can be had that are good for twenty-eight days. Many Canadians obtain them from the Embassy of the Union of Myanmar—the *M* word—located on the ninth floor of an upscale Ottawa apartment building, where the secretive ambassador, Nyunt Tin, has a staff of only ten. This means, of course, that Canada has diplomatic relations with Burma, as it does, as a matter of policy, with all countries that are members of the United Nations. Canada's ambassador, however, doesn't actually work in Burma but, in a typically Canadian compromise, occupies a corner of the Australian embassy in Bangkok: enlightened hypocrisy.

There's a distinct possibility that the situation in Burma might improve soon. As I write this, in spring 2002, a special UN envoy has been in talks with the junta for the past year and a half, hoping to extract a promise that Suu Kyi will be included in the governing process somehow or at least excused from house arrest. At the moment Rangoon is implying that this result might actually be achieved, as Burma's economy is a shambles and the generals badly need western investment and also a means of defusing growing dissent and generally distracting the attention of critics. Can such changes be depended on to happen? Of course not. If they do take place, can we predict their real effect? No.

Such are some of the reasons I wanted to go to Burma, ones that I felt outweighed the nomenclature question. As for getting there on my budget, the rusty old ship to Tahiti, followed by use of my cunningly hoarded frequent-flyer points from there to Bangkok, seemed the sole recourse.

Tunis is only seven hundred and twenty-six nautical miles from Piraeus, a three-day crossing at worst, weaving past the outlines of

Hellenic islands. By the end of the second day, a large-scale revolt broke out among a substantial portion of the passengers. People travelling as couples had been assigned cabins separate from one another, while pairs of men, unconnected in any way, mistakenly had been told to share a cabin with a single bed. Bernadette and I were contented enough, with our bathroom basin that leaked puddles of water on the historic floor and the dead insects ground into the walls like fruit flies embedded in amber. But most of the others seemed upset.

Their anger came to a head at the captain's cocktail party, that nautical tradition that closely tracks the first lifeboat drill. People were vocally angry, demanding immediate action and even rebates. The captain, a dramatic-looking Greek authority figure dressed for the occasion in a burgundy uniform with enormous epaulets and considerable piping, did what captains always do when trouble's brewing. He announced that drinks were on the house. Meanwhile, elsewhere on the ship, extra teams of workers were laying carpet and painting and replumbing and frantically rewiring electrical circuits. By the following day, the collective mood had improved somewhat, though we were taking an awfully long time crossing the Mediterranean. Part of our sloth was due to the fact that the ship had lost contact with the GPS satellite and actually had to retrace part of the route in order to find it again.

The old port of Tunis is distinguished by tangled streets of low stucco buildings with blue shutters and doors. The new part has less charm. Bernadette and I decided to get off the ship and go to Morocco, spending five days there touring around. Then we would meet up with the vessel (in the nick of time, we hoped) at Casablanca, from where it headed farther into the North Atlantic to the Canaries and the Cape Verde Islands on its way to South America.

What can one say of Casablanca except that the Rotary Club meets every third Thursday at the El Kandara Hotel at a time chosen so as not to conflict with the call to prayer? If Rick's Café Américain had ever actually existed, it now would be an Internet bar. It would be full not of refugees but rather of aimless young people (seventy percent of Moroccans are under thirty) and prosperous local business folk. The two go together to create terrible rush hours, driving back and forth between the city centre and new suburbs with names such as Californie, between the ocean-hugging core and the new Mohammed V Airport to the south. Such American-sounding names as Californie are popular in Casablanca and are used indiscriminately, as with a restaurant called Hollywood Tex Mex that offers neither a cinematic motif nor Tex-Mex cuisine. Anyway, the rush hours are so bad that police, instead of constantly rounding up the usual suspects, use bullhorns to tell drivers when to stop and let pedestrians cross.

Although no longer topical, the atmosphere of Michael Curtiz's 1942 film *Casablanca* was true to the Second World War period when Franklin Roosevelt, Charles de Gaulle, and Winston Churchill met in Anfa, just west of the central district. Casablanca was indeed a polyglot place, full of people trying to escape Nazi-dominated Europe. The mystic philosopher Simone Weil, for example, found herself there with no way to reach Lisbon and thence England. Freedom must have seemed so tantalizingly close. Gibraltar is reachable in only two hours by slow ferry, for instance. There was, however, never any such document as a "letter of transit." That's pure Hollywood invention. So is the notion that Casablanca is in the desert (Humphrey Bogart's character was incorrect in saying that he was misinformed on that point). Whatever trace or sense memory of those days remains is bound up with the fact that French civilization is still dominant.

When the French colonized Casablanca by force in 1912, at the start of the fifty-year French Protectorate period, the population was only about twenty thousand. The French were responsible for making Casablanca the busy place it has become. Virtually everyone speaks French as well as Arabic. By its look, the local commercial architecture, like every other form of culture, betrays its debt to the old days. Some landmarks, such as the old walled medina, with its spice sellers and bathhouses, predate the arrival of the French but they are dwarfed by modernity. Virtually no trace remains of the Portuguese, who preceded the French but left in the mid-eighteenth century after driving the Berber pirates out of Anfa.

Casablanca, which has nearly three million people, or more than a quarter of the country's urban population, is divided into five prefectures, each with its magnificent Moorish office building with scented courtyards and the anachronistic sound of clacking typewriters. The easiest way to get around is by public transport. There are both first-class and second-class buses as well as first- and second-class taxis. First-class taxis are secondhand Mercedes, a minimum eight years old, and take only one passenger each or one couple at a time. The others are *petits taxis*, battered red Peugeots that carry three or four or five or six unrelated customers, so that some resemble the little circus cars from which countless clowns emerge. Such European automobiles are assembled in Morocco, in Casablanca particularly, which is the country's industrial as well as financial capital even though not the seat of government. You see more expensive vehicles as well—more and more each year—but very few American ones, which are considered too large for any but the grand boulevards and too expensive to buy and operate. When we were there, gasoline was about forty-five US cents a litre, benzene about ninety. All of it is imported from the Middle East at a present cost of at least US$1 billion a year.

Casablanca is badly polluted from traffic during the two rush hours (much less so during the long afternoon siesta), but it's still an elegant, attractive, and sophisticated city. It makes a big display of its devoutness. Its most prominent building is the Hassan II Mosque, second in importance, it is said, only to al Haramaans in Mecca itself. Locally it's considered a marvel of marble and craftsmanship, on seventy-six hectares, with a minaret approximately two hundred metres high, overlooking the esplanade and the pounding Atlantic surf beyond. More than six thousand craftspeople took years to build it, working most of the time on 1980s landfill, though you would never know that now. Just beyond, the port is constantly full of ships—incoming tankers and outbound break-bulk vessels carrying phosphate (Morocco has ninety percent of the world's reserves). The phosphate mines, another legacy of French colonialism, export to Europe and America for fertilizer and chemical extraction. Yet Casablanca also has the most stylish shops, the greatest concentration of *boîtes de nuit*, the cream of French deco and moderne architecture, and a level of tolerance and sophistication not found anywhere else in Morocco, or possibly anywhere else in the Muslim world.

Guides and guidebooks usually emphasize that women perhaps enjoy more freedom in Morocco than in most other Islamic countries. This is a complicated comparison, but to the extent that the assertion is so, it's especially true in Casablanca, which presents itself as the country's liberal face, one seldom covered by a veil. At the slightest provocation people will point out that Casablanca boasts nine churches, a cathedral, and several synagogues, in addition to a hundred mosques, and has made great strides in eliminating the old slums called *bidonvilles*. If speaking candidly, locals might also tell you the obvious: that Casablancans, though devout, are not obsessively observant of every single religious prohibition, as is obvious from the way bars and casinos abound. These have such names as Zoom-Zoom, L'Ecume des Nuits, and Le Tube. Morocco produces excellent wine, which is gaining acceptance in the United States especially. Prostitution is more open in Casablanca than in other such moderate Muslim cities, though in Casablanca, typically, it seems to be carried out with a kind of well-dressed and well-bred discretion. People from Saudi Arabia, Iran, and the United Arab Emirates and others from even stricter places come to Casablanca to shop and indulge themselves.

"I certainly seem to be a sexual curiosity here," said Bernadette, referring to her red hair and green eyes and the kind of translucent skin that goes with them. There was no fear or malice in her remark, which was more sociological in tone. I wasn't surprised then, when returning from a self-directed tour of French deco and contemporary architecture, I found her sitting in the hotel lobby having a drink with a powerful-looking Arab man of about fifty. I didn't want to stumble into the conversation, so I withdrew to another area of the vast, empty lobby. Later she gave me the lowdown.

"Believe it or not," she said, "that was the head of the drug police in Libya." They share certain professional interests. The difference is that Bernadette labours at defending needle users, and the General, as we called him, works hard at persecuting them. She works with two other people; he has a staff of two thousand, with guns.

"He's lived in Casablanca for eight years," she told me. "He got a Ph.D. in criminology at one of the universities here." There are two such institutions in the city, both well regarded academically. "He's back now visiting for a few days after a conference in Berlin."

Apparently the two of them had been discussing criminal matters when I almost intruded.

"He said that the penalty for trafficking is fifteen years and for possessing enough to deal, three years. I asked him, 'What about the poor simple addict who's not doing anybody harm but himself?' He said, 'Such a person should simply come and talk to me.' I assume he meant he should turn informer."

Bernadette and the General debated two theories of drugs. "He thought full legalization wouldn't work. He pointed out how the Swiss have had to close their famous drug park. He said that First World countries always try to make the drug trade into a Third World problem."

The General also told her: "It's all about money with them, not immorality."

He also explained he would be in Casablanca for three more days. Bernadette replied she would be away, travelling to Marrakech, Fès, and Rabat, weaving in and out the Mid Atlas and the High Atlas Mountains. He then said he visited often from Libya and that, in any event, "Tripoli is another historical city you would enjoy." She thanked him politely. Then, *very* politely but *very* firmly, she finished her drink, crossed the floor, and took me by the arm and into the garden to recount the story excitedly. There are still some characters in Casablanca yet perhaps. Maybe with diligence one might even find a white dinner jacket hanging in a closet somewhere.

Bernadette and I had been hoping to have an intimate night together in Casablanca, but for various reasons—the memory of the General among them, I'm sure—she consumed an entire bottle of wine at dinner and picked an argument with me instead. The sun took every calorie of warmth with it when it descended at about 1800 hours, and the room had only a cold register and a broken thermostat. We spent the night under the covers in our trousers, shirts, and pullovers. She was in no mood to share body heat, and I'm not certain either of us had any to spare.

We made the long, hot drive to Marrakech, somehow expecting, against all actuarial logic, that it would still be filled with hippies. In fact, all the hippies are now either in Old Hippies' Homes or worrying about their mutual funds or agonizing about their waistlines. Yet making this slow journey southward about two hundred and fourteen kilometres, halfway to Algeria, not only disabused us of past stereotypes but also taught us a great deal about the lives of Morocco's twenty-six million people. For example, sixty-five percent of them work in agriculture, mainly of the subsistence sort, though the products are wide-ranging. There is a variety of orange, its fruit too bitter to eat, that is used only to produced marmalade (and its flowers to make tea). From November through March flowers are a big crop, mostly for export to Europe. You actually pass oases along the way—and thousands of sheep. Shepherdesses work the flocks without the help of dogs, which cost money. Instead they throw stones at the sheep to move them this way or that, just as in biblical times. Women haul water from wells with wooden windlasses; men work the fields with crude wooden ploughs pulled by donkeys or mules. In August, when the date palms are harvested, the temperature reaches forty-five degrees Celsius. Irrigation makes some kinds of wheat and other grains possible.

Marrakech, the old Berber capital, is in the High Atlas. Only as recently as 1955 was it served by the first charter flight from the United States. The route was the work of an entrepreneur who worked at one of the American military bases, the first of which was founded in 1941 to help fight in the North African theatre of the Second World War. The base closed in 1969 when the resources were needed on the other side of the world. Only at that point—after the base closures and during the Vietnam misunderstanding—did the influx of hippies begin.

From antediluvian tradition, rather than from any modern threats, the essence of Moroccan architecture is military. High walls surround nearly every farmstead no matter how poor. Much thicker and higher walls, usually crenellated and loopholed with arrow slots in the tower sides to permit enfilading fire, surround the cities. Marrakech is typical. Entering by highway or rail, you first pass through the prosperous but fairly ordinary-looking nouvelle ville, then through a small somewhat older middle phase sometimes referred to by Moroccans (not pejoratively, as far as I could tell) as "the Jewish quarter." Then come the high walls of the Old City. In this case, the walls date from our twelfth century. The whole complex together houses between one million and one and a half million people. All of the symptoms of modernity are present. For example, there is the avenue du Président Kennedy that one seems to find in all francophone cities everywhere. There is also La Mamouniz Hotel, which by tradition makes the list of everyone's great stately hotels of the world. Winston Churchill first discovered it following the Casablanca Conference with Roosevelt and de Gaulle in 1943. After that he would retreat there from time to time to paint and relax.

The hotel lies almost literally in the shadow of the royal palace walls. Given that Morocco, like China, has had so many dynasties, and so many princes as well as kings to house in splendour, nearly all the cities of any size have been capitals at one time or another. Palaces abound.

The drivers of petits taxis and the almost equally numerous pony-drawn calèches charge one set of fares for driving outside the Old City and another within. No wonder. The approach to the Old City is a huge square filled with snake charmers, jugglers, pantomime artists, political ranters, camels, bootblacks, storytellers in folk attire, and dentists *sans diplôme* who extract teeth on the spot *sans* anesthetic or painkillers. These are in addition to what is perhaps the world's densest concentration of pickpockets. Within the walls the city is medieval, the streets, paved with ancient stones, mimicking the meandering paths of animals now dead a millennium or more. Bernadette and I, feeling quite a bit more positive about each other now, returned by calèche to the hotel we had found. The rhythmic clatter of the pony's hooves changed pitch as we left the district of cobbled streets and entered the era of tarmac and concrete.

There is much in Muslim countries, even relatively liberal Morocco, to make western women (and men) grind their teeth in dismay and disgust. All day I could see Bernadette holding her tongue, not an action that comes to her easily (which is one of the reasons I like her so much). Now this enforced restraint of being a guest in public places was coming to an end. I leaped out first, taking her hand and helping her reach the running board and then the curb. Once inside the hotel room she was perfectly free to let off steam. "This is barbaric," she kept saying. But not for long. We had to be up and away early to commence the long trip to Fès in the Mid Atlas, a day-and-night journey to one of the three holiest cities in Islam (after Jerusalem and Mecca, of course), founded in 808 by a sixth-generation descendant of Mohammed.

Fès is usually so spelled so as to distinguish it from fez, the hat, more properly called a tarboosh, which is no longer much worn, as it is seen as a symbol of Turkish domination. Fès was Morocco's first capital. Its old walled quarter, Fès el Bali, is often said to be the best-preserved living medieval city, famous for its medina, which is broken up into souks or markets, one for every kind of commodity or service. There is no accurate map of the souks. You simply hire a knowledge-able guide or wander about by yourself, hopeful of somehow, someday, stumbling on one of the gates that lead outside. This area is huge (the walls have fourteen gates) and is full of the koranic schools called *medersas* as well as every variety of small shop.

Getting to Fès is an instructive ordeal. Along the winding two-lane highway are olive groves and potato patches and also grain fields that yield between two and four crops a year. The soil varies from rich coffee-coloured to a rusty red. With urging everything seems to grow: paprika, sugar beets, flowers. The one visible luxury engaged in by the small farms is growing a eucalyptus tree. A luxury because a mature tree, with roots twenty to forty metres long, requires three hundred and twenty litres of water a day: a formidable demand even in Fès itself, which receives water from not one but two mountain ranges.

As we approached, we saw a small group of Bedouin milling about their black tents. In modern times they are only seminomadic people, living at a fixed location in a permanent dwelling most of the year, but ranging about with their sheep as necessary, following the grass. Nor are they so polygamous as they once were. Each adult Bedouin male now has only two wives: a young one who travels with him, an older one who remains behind with the family. Bernadette, whom I admire partly because she's a champion of the underdog who nonetheless despises victim culture and the language of political correctness, seemed to wince and shrug at the same time—wince at the inequality, shrug at the inevitability. Through some fundamental last-minute packing problem, she had been wearing more or less the same clothes for about a week, but now, with the sun so bright and her skin so fair, she had added a wide-brimmed floppy straw hat, but needed it only a few hours. At 1730 hours the sun fell out of the sky like a drunken actor toppling into the orchestra pit. No dusk, no gradual fading of detail, just boom and then absolute darkness, which brought out the animals of the night—and the soldiers and police.

Mohammed VI had succeeded to the throne only about a hundred days earlier, on the death of his beloved and feared father, Hassan II. The new king was in residence at Fès that night, and this fact occasioned numerous roadblocks and checkpoints along the highway leading to the city. But something more was afoot as well. For the last twenty years of his reign, Hassan II's favourite tough guy, adviser, and golfing partner (the monarch made many of his decisions on the links) was Driss Basri, interior minister and security chief. Basri knew his days in power were numbered, as in recent years he had supported Mohammed VI's brother, Crown Prince Moulay Rachid, for the monarchy. What's more, Basri was the person Moroccans blamed for the country's unusual elections, general corruption, and exuberant secret police, for to blame the monarch for such ills was unthinkable. Shortly after the coronation, a mysterious fire destroyed the security police archives. In the old days Basri would have been beheaded. As it was, Mohammed removed him from power much more quickly than anyone had expected, but the situation hadn't quite settled down. There still might be units loyal to Basri roaming the countryside with the sheep.

Soon enough we saw Fès off on the horizon, a low string of bright lights extending miles to the north and south. The spectacle seemed to keep receding the farther we drove. Finally we arrived in the nouvelle ville to find what the streetlamps revealed: that the pavements along at least the big thoroughfares were paved with squares of Italian marble. This didn't seem to be a product of the French Protectorate period (1912–56), which was responsible for the magnificent boulevards themselves; rather it was a taste of

Moroccan nationalism. In any event, the nouvelle ville is not what beckoned us but rather the Mellah, the old Jewish quarter once full of goldsmiths and salt dealers, and the ageless Medina, which is a labyrinth of small shops. Thanks to old movies, westerners believe that casbah (more properly, kasbah) refers to just such a maze of alleyways off alleyways, so complex that no map can ever be made of them, so full of shadows and secrets that only criminals, probably ones born with such knowledge, can live there, free from police interference. In fact, a kasbah is merely an old fort, built, often by one of the monastic orders, to protect the city it overlooks: a citadel in fact. The kasbah in Rabat, the new capital chosen by the French in 1912, is the perfect example. It contains no medina and no souks. The old walled part of Fès, however, perfectly matches the Hollywood definition.

The high ochre walls and elaborate gates date from our fourteenth century when Fès was already the intellectual capital of Morocco, as it still purports to be. Fès has about 1.7 million people. Roughly three hundred thousand, half of them artisans, live within the medina walls, eighty percent upstairs over their shops. Rentals become available rarely. The medina has electricity and telephones, but transport is by donkey and mule. The animals stagger through the narrow cobbled streets carrying loads that sometimes seem too big for the space through which they must pass. Some of the streets have stone runnels to carry out the waste.

Many of the shopkeepers—too many, though a small percentage of the total—are merely dealers in tourist junk. There are places to buy Céline Dion posters and Toronto Blue Jays jackets. Most of the tiny stalls sit in the heat, some shaded by mats of dry grasses laid from one rooftop to another. Walking the stones burnished by millions of shuffling feet, one sees herbalists, dealers in pelts and skins, chicken decapitators, numismatists, gravestone carvers, cabinet makers, ivory turners, jewellery designers, metalsmiths, people whose sole livelihood is making bellows, and the rather disturbing individuals who spend their lives cleaving open the heads of sheep and pulling out the brains in long strands. And, of course, there are carpets, both Berber and oriental, double-stitched and simply woven, all in almost infinite variety. The carpet makers are unique, as far as we could determine, in operating as a cooperative within the medina, where a sumptuous series of display rooms is overseen by a jovial band of smooth-talking salesmen, who pour the mint tea freely and speak the American idiom almost perfectly.

Another famous specialty of the medina at Fès is the djelabba, the ubiquitous long hooded garment worn over street clothes. I had looked for one my size in Casablanca and Marrakech, only to be disappointed in the fit and the workmanship. In Fès, where craft standards are higher, I was rewarded for my patience. I wished such a garment because I was tired both of sleeping in my clothes on cold desert evenings or shivering all night without them. A high-quality woolen djelabba, hand-sewn, seemed the perfect nightshirt. After considerable haggling in his miniscule back office, a tailor sold me one at what I thought a reasonable price. To cinch the deal he threw in free *babouches* for my feet. I chose a pair in bright yellow leather, as these are traditionally reserved for the notarial classes: scribes, clerks, copyists, writers of letters on behalf of the illiterate.

We drove the short distance from Fès to Meknes, a pleasant market town that is the service centre for a wide agricultural area, and from there at last to Rabat, a city that, as befits a national capital, has numerous official landmarks, such as the Great Mosque, the Hassan Tower, and the Mausoleum of Mohammed V. The first of these is actually across the languid river, so technically in the city of Salé. Rabat was chosen as the capital because of its accommodating Mediterranean harbour, a far more protected and attractive one to French eyes than Casablanca's on the North Atlantic. These days, however, the port's importance for most ordinary people is less than that of the large motorway linking the two places. We followed this autobahn for half a day and picked up our ship in Casablanca with hours to spare.

CEMITÉRIO
DOS ELEFANTES

As a favour to his friends, the ship's owners, a former admiral in the Greek navy had come aboard to deal with some of the complaints his pals had been hearing. He stayed a few days, only long enough to perform such tasks as firing the hospitality director. He turned the library, already a haven for bridge players, into a meeting hall for "friends of Bill Wilson" (code for Alcoholics Anonymous) and transformed one of the few sizable open spaces into a casino, with roulette, twenty-one, and long rows of slots. One of his final acts before disembarking was to isolate a known American troublemaker, a kind of self-proclaimed guru who kept trying to organize the unhappy passengers into a sort of union. The Greek confined the fellow to a table all by himself in the dining room. The dining room was constantly producing these bizarre characters. One, named Chip, a huge former bill collector, muscular and heavily tattooed, used any provocation to give people his business card, which announced his candidacy for the US presidency as a single-taxer and champion of a national four-day work week. When he wasn't campaigning on land or sea, Chip travelled America in an RV with a Harley-Davidson in the back.

Tenerife in the Canary Islands was our next stop. In Bernadette's assessment it was "worse than Torremolinos." It's the largest centre and most populous of the Canaries, whose others include Isla de la

Gran Canaria, immediately to the east, where the body of the rogue Fleet Street publisher Robert Maxwell washed ashore in 1984. Close as it is to North Africa, there are few Arabs in Tenerife but plenty of British and German expats. The sort of people whose grandparents were lucky to get an annual seaside holiday at Brighton now have condos in this compact and unattractive Spanish city—full name, Santa Cruz de Tenerife—whose edges are traced in black volcanic sand. The traveller sees a rising tide of nationalism everywhere these days; Tenerife is no exception. Hoardings, buildings, and rock faces are spray-painted with messages championing this or that political party, all of them denouncing Spanish colonialism. The main problems are that there are many more cars than the environment can absorb, and too few jobs to support the 1.5 million or so residents. Francisco Franco, who used the Canaries as a base from which to build the coup that made him Spain's president, erected an oil refinery there, which employs six thousand people. Without it the Canaries would be left with tourism and bananas. The refinery is a hot potato politically. Unofficially unemployment is put as high as forty percent. The first action taken by male youths who manage to find a job, any job, is to buy an automobile on credit, in order to acquire a girlfriend in the bargain.

Some interesting work is being done in archaeology, though this is not yet obvious in local institutions such as the Museo Militarde Almeyda, where the most famous display is of the cannon that tore away Lord Nelson's arm. An American team is investigating ancient pyramidal structures to determine whether they provide any link between the pyramid cultures of Mexico and Egypt—an idea not so farfetched as it sounds when one studies a map of the ocean currents. There's a lot going on in Canarian architecture too. A now completed convention centre and a concert hall still under construction when we were there are both important expressions of a native Canary Islands style, influenced by the Spanish who have dominated and destroyed it since the fifteenth century. These days, however,

Tenerife is cannibalizing itself—a very different problem from that of the Cape Verde Islands, another four hundred or so nautical miles out in the Atlantic.

If the Canaries are seen as part of North Africa, then the Cape Verde Islands are part of West Africa, in that they lie six hundred kilometres or so off Senegal and the visitor sees children with bellies swollen by starvation. We arrived in the port city of Praia São Tiago at 0700, and spent hours fighting the bureaucracy to get ashore. We fell in with a young Cape Verdean named Alexander who had the initial *A* tattooed on one forearm with a stencil. He wished to use us to practise his English, which was indeed in a poor state of repair. Cape Verde was a colony of Portugal for four hundred years, until 1975, and the tongues spoken are Portuguese and the local creole called Crioulu. His very limitation with English frequently gave A's speech a wonderfully pithy eloquence. "When it rain like this year, times are good," he said, gesturing to indicate small patches of stunted green trees beyond the dust-choked streets full of crumbling cottages and bone-dry riverbeds filled with discarded tires and other rubbish. "But once it did not rain for ten years. Yes, ten years. Many times, three years." There's little *verde* in Cape Verde.

The civil police and the military were everywhere in town, the only well-clad and well-shod citizens we saw. The latter had a battery of cannon in front of their headquarters. Aside from a Chinese general store, the buildings with the most activity buzzing round them were the offices of rival political parties. Here too many flat surfaces were covered in political graffiti, but unlike those in Tenerife, they were painted in uneven, scraggly alphabets—written hurriedly and truncated abruptly when cops were heard coming round the corner. The most beautiful object in Praia São Tiago was a new thirty-metre teak schooner from the United States, nodding gently at anchor. Next to it was the recent wreck of a similarly expensive wooden yacht, lines still dangling from its spars, which stuck above the surface like television aerials in a 1950s cityscape.

Historically the main export of Cape Verde has been its own people. Forcibly so, in the days of the slavers, who used the island as an entrepôt for their grisly trade. Eagerly so, later, when Cape Verdeans proved themselves expert sailors and especially harpooners, much in demand by the whaling trade during the first few decades of the nineteenth century. Remittances from expats are still what keep the economy going (that and the fact that Cape Verde's telecommunications system is used for much of the world's phone-sex industry). "To get to Europe or America or Brazil and find work is what everybody—all my friends—dream," said A. "It is very difficult, but there is no other way for any of us."

Except for several offshore banks and one Mercedes, most of Praia São Tiago looks to date from the earlier half of the Portuguese occupation, but Praia is the New Town. A offered to guide us to the old town, Cidade Velha, on the other side of the island. It still looks precisely as Charles Darwin describes in 1831 at the very beginning of *The Voyage of the Beagle*. Horrified by the slave ships in the harbour of what he called Porto Praya, but seeming to enjoy his first glimpse of a tropical location, young Darwin and two of the ship's officers "hired mounts and rode to Ribeira Grande, a village a few miles eastward.... [U]ntil we reached the village of St Martin, the county presented its usual dull brown appearance; but here, a very small rill of water produces a most refreshing margin of luxuriant vegetation. In the course of an hour we arrived at Ribeira Grande, and were surprised at the sight of a large ruined fort and cathedral. This little town, before its harbour was filled up, was the principal place of the island: it now presents a melancholy, but very picturesque appearance. Having procured a black padre for a guide, and a Spaniard who had served in the Peninsular War as an interpreter, we visited a collection of buildings, of which an ancient church formed the principal part. It is here the governors and captain-generals of the islands have been buried. Some of the tombstones recorded dates of the sixteenth century [*sic*—in fact, the fifteenth]."

Little has changed. Certainly little has improved. From Darwin's description you can easily recognize the ragtag fishing village of a few score dwellings, some barely standing, not all of them occupied, at least not by humans. Goats and chickens live in some. So do lizards, especially in the lime-washed tower of the old church, which I thought at first might have been a dovecote (it has that shape) but knew was the original belfry when Bernadette and I ventured up the circular stairs and saw the blue ceramic tiles called *tadeo azulejos*. The village and its harbour—still silted over—were protected by the enormous masonry fortress, the Muro Baracä e Fosso Seco. It too looks as Darwin described it in the 1830s, with its black volcanic rock, white fieldstone, and orange tile. The structure, which took two hundred years to build, sits at the wide end of a site shaped like a slice of cake. On one side of the triangle there's a straight drop to the sea maybe two hundred metres below; on the second, an unbridgeable canyon with walls just as high and steep. The only means of attack was across many kilometres of barren and incredibly thirsty land, too rocky even for goats to navigate, but with rocks too small to provide cover for humans. This side was the most strongly defended one, with outerworks to further hinder any approach. The fort is one of the most impressive pieces of military engineering I've ever seen and could scarcely have been taken by stealth or storm.

Standing on the parapets, looking out over a field where old iron cannon lay in a pile like stove wood, I heard the crow of roosters waft up from the hamlet, which seemed picturesque from such an eminence. Up close it seemed otherwise—full of poor, poor people with no hopes and no prospects. Bernadette pointed out that if they had delayed independence for only a couple of decades they would now be reaping equalization benefits from the European Union. We were standing in the original plaza in the shadow of the cathedral. In the centre of the square is an old stone whipping post with iron rings and bars, used to punish slaves. A number of friendly citizens had gathered out of curiosity. Bernadette asked, "Why do they wave at us? Why don't they spit at us?" Okay, this may not be everyone's idea of paradise, but I like the lonely, rocky places—islands ideally— where just by existing you rid the mind of so much superfluous nonsense and life seems to reprioritize itself. That evening, at about 2200, the ship went aground briefly in the silty bottom of the harbour at Praia, which the government, unaccustomed to deep-draught vessels, can't afford to dredge. A tug freed us easily, and we set out into the Atlantic, heading southwest across the Equator, one thousand nine hundred and ninety-five nautical miles from Salvador da Bahia, the most African city in Brazil, a passage of nine days and eight nights.

The voyage was not turning out as everyone had envisioned but simply as the most pessimistic had feared. The ship had lived fast but long, though personally I felt only comfort in sleeping below the waterline in a vessel commissioned before I was born: the comfort of being with history (and the knowledge that ships are better built than people). The vessel, which rode the weather well, had three-stage steam turbines, converted to diesel, though by looking at coaming-like marks on the engine room's deck plates, you could see where the stokers had stood to shovel coal. What was wrong was that the plumbing and ventilation were falling apart, seeming at first to ignite what the ship's doctor admitted was a serious epidemic of upper-respiratory illness that was all he could handle. I would estimate that ninety percent of the passengers were down with it at one time or another. I was among the first and sickest.

Black stuff like creosote kept falling from the ceilings in certain cabins while others had two or three inches of water sloshing over the carpets. Such hardships were particularly difficult for the groups of seniors who made up most of the passengers when the fit, younger L. L. Bean types, advertised for with such splash in the North American (but not apparently the European) press, failed in droves to respond to the allure of Christmas in Antarctica. One poor woman lay bedfast for six days in a cabin without a working toilet and was forced to use the wastepaper basket as a chamber pot. When she recovered her mobility, she left the ship in disgust, at Rio, I believe. Others defected as well. Yet in fairness I must say that most such people were unsophisticated whiners who were expecting reality to emulate *The Love Boat*. The complex education programmes designed by the creators of the voyage went largely unutilized by loud North Americans who couldn't be troubled even to read a guidebook. One night at dinner I called the most uncultured ones so many hillbillies, and Bernadette took me to task.

"Look, these are just poor people who've always dreamed of going round the world, or at least having a couple of months of being able to eat lobster and not have to cook and have people wait on them for a change. I was talking to a woman who came out of retirement and worked for two years to get the money to pay for this trip."

I felt chastised. Or at least I kept my derogatory labels to myself. I also found that on closer examination, scattered here and there among the hillbillies and Okies, were a few cosmopolites, such as a supposed Polish countess. In any case, the management was more laughable than the passengers. In the continuing mix-up about cabin assignment, two sixty-year-old males, an American and a Canadian, strangers to each other, found themselves sharing a room. When the American arrived back drunk late one night, with a female companion in a similar condition, the Canadian refused to leave as requested. Threats ensued. The Canadian pulled a knife. A new place had to be found for the American. The next morning's intercom announcements included a plea for passengers to turn in all offensive weapons until completion of the voyage.

A shipping executive from Taipei just happened to be aboard, travelling with his family. Being an old Taiwan hand, I engaged him in conversation. "This could be a special ship if the people involved were prepared to spend the necessary amount of money," he said, looking sadly at the surroundings. "I will say this—the seamanship is faultless as far as I can tell."

During the passage from Cape Verde to Salvador da Bahia, we saw no other ships, though the last two days after we started hugging the coast and passed the mouth of the Amazon there were many distant islands and lighthouses on the headlands and, of course, assorted species of booby and other seabirds. So we awoke at dawn on our twentieth day at sea to find the ship berthed in Salvador. We were perhaps at the very spot we eventually would have reached anyway, because of the current that flows from Cape Verde to there: a most important current indeed. It formed the basis of the Portuguese empire and was one of the key factors in the slave trade, just as the Portuguese colony at Goa in India was the terminus of the current that carried them there from Africa.

We were now approaching the ides of December, and in Salvador, where the temperature was expected to reach thirty-seven degrees Celsius, the shops were preparing for the rush of Christmas business. One of the main squares had been decorated with two enormous Santas, one caucasian, the other African. This seemed highly symbolic, necessary, and entirely appropriate. What is true of Brazil generally, compared with other places, is especially true of Bahia state and Salvador its capital: that although the Portuguese introduced slavery there in the 1560s, and although slavery remained legal as late as 1888, there is no die-hard racial hatred even approaching that familiar to Americans, for example. The reason, briefly stated, is that the infant US republic was quick to ban the importation of slaves from Africa but slow to abolish slavery (and only then, of course, after civil war). The result was to turn the slavers from importers to smugglers and, much more important, to change plantations into breeding stations. Miscegenation, much less racial intermarriage, was a serious illegality in most of the United States, north as well as south, until comparatively recent times—a legacy of the idea that the precious stock of slaves must not be denatured. In Brazil the approach was different. The life of a slave brought from the Guinea coast or, later, Angola was no picnic to be sure, but many could and did buy their freedom. And intermarriage between Africans and Portuguese was commonplace. For generations, in fact, mulattos (a term derogatory from the beginning, coming from the word for mule) were Salvador's high society. Today between eighty and eighty-three percent of Bahians have at least some African blood. Most everyone, in other words, is somewhat black, somewhat European, probably somewhat aboriginal in descent. To the outsider from places with greater racial problems than Brazil's, this all seems to have worked out fine.

One underlying cause of such overall harmony was the Roman Catholic Church, which adopted and adapted many of the elements of the African religions. The result is today's Candomblé, which blends the Christian variety of meditation with the importance of trances, and worships ancestors as well as saints. A belief in an actual God, who takes a hand in life's daily outcomes, is another contribution from the African side of the ledger, as is the importance of symbolic sacrifice, usually of children. The most significant place of worship in Salvador da Bahia is St. Francis of Assisi Cathedral. With its one tonne of gold leaf, it's said to be the third richest church in the world, after St. Peter's in Rome and Our Lady of Guadalupe in Mexico City. How appropriate that one of the saints looking down on celebrants from a carving should be St. Benedictus (not to be confused with St. Benedict of the Benedictines). Benedictus was a fifteenth-century man of colour, son of an Italian father and a mother who was an Egyptian slave. He is the patron saint of singers. Closer inspection of the cathedral shows some African masks among the walls of sacred carved panels, in place now for nearly five hundred years. As in religion, so in gastronomy. Plain old Portuguese cod long ago became an African fish stew called *moqueca*, flavoured with coconut milk.

Like all such old cities, Salvador da Bahia has had its ups and downs economically. It was the capital until 1763, for example. The strata can be traced in its many layers of churches from different periods, and of forts; for when it was richest it most needed protection. One fort has an abandoned Dutch foundation that the Portuguese didn't finish off until much later, in the eighteenth century, when trade was booming. Cycles of fortune affected the religious orders as well. The Benedictines, the Franciscans, and the Jesuits were all influential at various times. Some still own much property, including, in the case of the Franciscans, an art deco cinema of all things. The Jesuits were expelled eventually (their fate in so many places) for, among other reasons, their refusal to allow the indigenous people to be enslaved. Salvador's most glorious boom took place in 1808 when the Portuguese royal family and the nobility, fleeing Napoleon's invasion of the Iberian peninsula, removed themselves to Salvador for a few months before moving on for a long stay in Rio de Janeiro. They left much valuable infrastructure behind them.

At the time Salvador consisted of a town perched on a steep cliff overlooking the harbour defences. But an outbreak of plague in 1826 caused many to flee to sea level seventy metres below. The result is that today Salvador is a two-tiered city geographically as well as economically. The rich get richer and the poor even poorer, and the middle class is squeezed to eventual extinction. Many of the wealthy live on one side of the topmost layer of rock, with private funiculars to take them from their houses to the yachts on private jetties on the Bay of All Souls. On the other long side of the isosceles triangle is the Pelorinho district (the word means whipping post— shades of Cape Verde). As recently as a decade ago, this area, celebrated by the novelist Jorge Amado, was all but synonymous with prostitution and drugs. Now it's synonymous with old architecture and new art (music and theatre especially), with cafés and galleries with handicrafts of often surprisingly high quality. Lapidaries and silversmiths, from some of the world's most famous to some of the least, sell from the front of their shops that which they make in workrooms in the back.

Only about twenty years ago Salvador had a population of approximately six hundred thousand; the figure now approaches three million. As it has ballooned in size, the city has gained in sophistication and quality of life. Few like to discuss one fact with strangers: how as late as a few years ago there were occasional outbreaks of cholera. Now the entire sanitation system has been rethought and redesigned. Bernadette and I had to spend time in town for some necessary shopping for ourselves and others. One fellow passenger's washbasin had a hole in it that she couldn't get fixed and asked us to be on the lookout for a small plastic tub, which we found in a supermarket, along with luxuriant and exotic soaps and the customary thieves preying on the customers. Otherwise we spent a long and exhausting day in Pelorinho, for the streets are cobbled and as steep as San Francisco's.

Most big cities on the sea long ago redeveloped their own waterfronts, relegating the maritime industry to new port facilities a discreet distance from the downtown shopping district. Rio de Janeiro is a half-exception. We went down the gangway and through the gate and found ourselves in the middle of the *centro*. The difference is that central Rio is simply no longer the city centre but a vast vandalized commercial slum full of half-razed or partially collapsed buildings, colonial as well as modern. Unique in my experience, buildings in Rio are defaced with graffiti not just at street level but also as high as the third or fourth storeys. This indicates a level of enterprise visible nowhere else in the old commercial hub.

Everyone says that the other slums of Rio—the residential ones, the hillside shantytowns called *favelas* where fifteen percent of the population live—are nowhere so poor and sad as they were only a decade ago. I was in no position to judge. Visitors also commonly learn that the rich, of course, have grown still richer, and this is easier to believe with one's eyes even on first acquaintance. The posh shopping areas are posh indeed. In fact, even a brief stop reveals that Rio enjoys, just as the cariocas always have claimed, a civic style all its own.

They will tell you that it is hedonistic and even sybaritic compared to that of pollution-bound and industrial São Paulo, eight hundred kilometres to the southwest, which generates a third of Brazil's gross domestic production and has one of the world's highest concentrations of civilian helicopters. If São Paulo has its way, it will soon have the world's tallest building as well, higher than the Petronas Towers in Kuala Lumpur.

Rio's attractions are justly famous. The Avenue Presidente Vargas, named for the most important dictator of the modern era, who put his stamp on Brazil as surely as his contemporary Franklin Roosevelt did on the United States, is impressively broad, even majestic. Rio is big and crowded and lacerated with freeways. Like the Interstate highway system in the United States, these freeways began as a military idea in disguise, designed to speed the city's evacuation in time of war; construction brought many of Rio's foremost Portuguese colonial buildings crashing down. As for Carnival, many cariocas, the candid ones, will you tell they now prefer the equivalent in Salvador da Bahia. In Salvador, in fact, there is an all-engaging city-wide festival every month. In general, though, cariocas are contemptuous of the northeast, regarding it as uncivilized back country, much as people in Melbourne and Sydney regard the tropical excesses of Queensland.

Then, of course, there are the beaches of Rio. The crowds of people there give Rio its reputation for self-involvement, not the throngs labouring in the bank towers in what locals call the Bermuda Triangle ("We see the investment go in, but then it disappears from the radar screens"). The beach people, with their perfect bodies shaped to contours fashionable in the 1950s, made me think of dinosaurs: bronzed reptiles of the Late Curvaceous Period. Copacabana, Ipanema, and Leblon are divided by common agreement into areas for the topless or the gay as well as for heterosexual couples and families. Gay men, who seem to favour a kind of volleyball-soccer called *futvolei*, appear far more numerous than topless women, though a book I read recently made me realize that Brazilian sexual preference is not always the matter of carefree expression it would seem, not even during Carnival. The most interesting beach is known as the *cemitério dos elefantes*, because it is the traditional hangout of old leftists, intellectuals, and hippies, especially those who in 1968 clashed with the military government of the time. People come to stare at them the way they stared at the now-repatriated Ronald Biggs, the Great Train Robber, not because he was a celebrity but rather because he was a curiosity from the past, an artefact.

Today's political activists, constantly protesting some facet of President Fernando Henrique Candosa's government in Brasilia, are more colourful. They include Magno Malta, a singing evangelist and former drug addict who, being a congressman, chaired a multiparty inquiry into the country's drug trade. This business is said to be centred in a shantytown down by Rio's port, where the commissioners were warned not to go for fear of being shot. The inquiry did result in charges against many people, including a fellow member of congress accused of dismembering an opponent with a chain saw.

Much has always been made of Rio's cosmopolitanism. There are certainly large foreign communities, Italian, Japanese, Jewish, complete in every particular. But I didn't see much evidence of culture-mixing, except once. Bernadette and I were walking down the Rua Visconde de Piraja going to the weekly "hippie fair," a vast open-air crafts and art sale that is mostly junk and has nothing to do with hippies except by the loose Brazilian definition: hippie equals bohemian pachyderm. Along the way we discovered that this was the day of the annual book fair in which booksellers, new and antiquarian, join with publishers in taking their wares to the streets for block after block. The Brazilian books were fascinating, so vibrant, so strongly designed. But what struck me most was the variety of current literature, philosophy, art, and psychology available in so many different languages. This bespoke a genuine cosmopolitanism not always so blatantly apparent. Yet compared to Buenos Aires, Rio is a big, overgrown beach town, a sort of Venice, California, on a giant scale.

Steaming down the coast to the Argentine capital—I love being able to use the verb *steaming* correctly for once—was a matter of a couple of days. The crucial point came off Uruguay when we passed the twinkling lights of Montevideo several nautical miles off, marking the wide estuary of the Rio de la Plata where the Nazi battleship *Graf Spree* was destroyed in the Second World War. Even the workaday port area of Buenos Aires was a charming blend of old and new, though this was the New Port, built for container shipping. The Old has been turned into a bohemian district with a few nods to the past, such as a ship chandler's in business there since 1859. Bernadette had to drag me away to keep me from buying Danforth anchors and other necessary souvenirs.

To call Buenos Aires the Paris of Latin America is worthless even as a cliché. Its superficially Parisian aspects—the gracious boulevards, the cathedrals, the elegant public buildings, and the grand opera house—are simply what one expects of South American capitals. Its soul seems more Italian than French. There appears to be more room there for the middle class than there is in Rio or the big cities of the north. One indication of this difference is the subway system, virtually useless for getting round the heart of the city, being instead a set of spokes radiating from a central station in order to service the suburbs. Indeed Buenos Aires has excellent public buses, to say nothing of an astonishing forty-five thousand taxis. About thirty-five thousand of them are legally licensed. All of them are clean, as far as I could judge by random sampling.

Buenos Aires lacks many of Rio's problems, such as the destructive freeways and the obstructive mountains (though, officially, the mountains are great civic virtues). It also lacks Rio's high level of murder and other violent crime. In Rio merchants hire mercenaries, some of them said to be off-duty cops, to kill street kids who lower the tone of Copacabana Beach. The main threat to careful tourists in Buenos Aires is mustard artists. These are pickpockets who first distract their marks by spilling condiments on them. Like Rio, Buenos Aires has played musical chairs with its neighbourhoods. Roughly speaking, the prosperous citizens live in the northern portions of the city, the poorer ones in the southern. The former areas include Palermo Chio, where houses worth US$3 to $4 million sit amid jacquarandas. Another such prosperous area is the Recoleta district, where businesses such as Sotheby's, Hermès, and Cartier are found. Every day of the week people keep hours traditional to the Argentine leisured classes, an eccentricity the middle class can afford only on weekends. Their rhythm might be characterized by having dinner at 2200 hours or later before visiting the discos or clubs, which open at 0130 hours, then enjoying a big breakfast at 0630 or so before going to bed. Until 1871 the wealthy lived in the south. That year a yellow fever epidemic drove them north, leaving the south deserted. In districts such as Recoleta professional dog walkers are conspicuous. They charge about one hundred US dollars a month to exercise twice daily the pets of people too busy to do so themselves. A popular dog walker may be seen perambulating twenty leashed clients at once.

Recoleta's principal sight, however, is its vast aboveground cemetery, opened in 1881 but containing the reinterred bodies of notables in all walks of death stretching back to the turn of the nineteenth century, their coffins visible through the doors of the square mausoleums, each more expensive-looking than the last. Rows of these make up a city of the dead, with long avenues, cross streets, and laneways. Aboveground burial is simply a cultural custom for those who can afford it, not a matter related to the watertable, as in New Orleans. Being newer and having less vegetation, Recoleta lacks the air of decrepit creepiness of Père Lachaise in Paris or Highgate in London. But you sometimes turn a corner to see carts stacked with the once costly caskets of generals and politicians who are, for some reason, being moved from one address to another. The shrouded contents sometimes poke out of the seams of the slowly decaying mahogany or rosewood boxes, and there is a slight but unmistakable whiff of human decomposition. The only person in Recoleta not entombed aboveground is the beloved dictatrix Evita. Eva Perón, who died of ovarian cancer in 1956 at the age of thirty-six, was more widely travelled in death than she was in life, her body being hidden in various locations round Buenos Aires (once, behind the screen in one of the big cinemas) before being exiled to Europe, where she enjoyed several years' burial in Italy. The corpse was finally returned to Argentina in 1976 during the reign of the last military government. It was placed under either six or nine metres of concrete (accounts vary) next to the tomb of her family. The spot has many commemorative bronze plaques and is never without anonymous fresh flowers. Evita is the person whose likeness one sees for sale most often on T-shirts and posters, even in life-size plaster busts. The face of Che Guevara is a close second. This twinning indicates the degree of polarization that still runs strongly through politics in the now once again democratic Republic of Argentina.

Once upon a time Argentina was as materially prosperous as, say, Canada. When its economic position began to erode, the way was paved for dictatorships. These favoured the new rich, leaving out the older, better-educated aristocracy with roots in European culture. Bernadette and I found vivid evidence of this time and again as we devoted a day to the antique shops clustered in San Telmo and other districts. The wealth and taste that once obtained in Buenos Aires! The crystal chandeliers, the furniture, the art, the books and manuscripts, the jewellery with stones cut in shapes that were fashionable before the Second World War—all quite unbelievable. Neither of us had ever seen a shop with an antique flatware service for forty, complete down to ice-cream spoons and lobster forks, made entirely of gold. Buenos Aires is far more subtle than Rio. Its society, being more complex, is less on display. A few famous obsessions, such as the tango, are ubiquitous and distract visitors from other aspects of life. Except perhaps during rush hour, the newcomer may not experience the seething rage, called *bronca*, to which it is said all true Buenos Aireans (*portenos*) are heir. Similarly the lucky guest may not notice the custom called *viveza criolla* (often translated as "artful living").

The best-known ritual in Buenos Aires takes place at 1500 each Thursday when the Mothers in White, also called the Women in White, take up their vigil in the Plaza de Mayo (Argentines pronounce it *Mazzo*) opposite the presidential palace, the Casa Rosanda. They are easily identified by their white scarves. Stencilled on the pavement are the white silhouettes of human forms. Both symbols represent the thirty thousand "disappeared ones," leftists and suspected intellectuals who simply vanished into unmarked graves—if that—in the junta crackdown that began in 1977. But this is no Argentine version of the elephants' graveyard. A new generation of women is continuing the protest, even through the military leaders were sentenced to life imprisonment in 1985 (and pardoned four years later). The movement's headquarters is now the café bookshop called Librería de las Madres. Curiously another place to learn about the peace movement is the Museo de Armas, the state military museum. There you can find displays, very carefully worded, dealing with the Falkland Islands conflict of 1982, Britain's last colonial war and some say its only noble one, as it resulted in Prime Minister Margaret Thatcher, that friend of such dictators as Augusto Pinochet of Chile, restoring democratic government to Argentina. Wishing to see the Falklands for ourselves, Bernadette and I reboarded the ship.

Title to the islands, which have been British in population and culture since the 1840s but lie only about four hundred and eight kilometres off the Argentine coast, had been in dispute throughout the intervening hundred and sixty years. Indeed, Argentines have been brought up to believe that the Islas Malvinas, as they're known in Spanish, are Argentine territory under British occupation. By 1982 the junta led by General Leopoldo Galtieri was facing increasing unrest. Reactions to years of repression were growing strong, and though inflation had recently declined to a mere one hundred percent from a high of three hundred, the generals felt they needed a short, successful military adventure, the sort favoured by American presidents, to renew patriotism and distract the people from their petty concerns. At 0600 on 2 April 1982, Argentine helicopters and landing craft deposited the first waves of troops on the ground. Some of the invaders were hardened veterans, but most were recent recruits, many literally picked up off the back streets of Buenos Aires only days or weeks earlier. The British governor, Rex Hunt, and eighty Royal Marines on the island put up a symbolic resistance and then were permitted to evacuate to a neutral third country: Paraguay. Argentina installed its own governor and administration and took control of communications and the airport. It threatened the residents with harsh reprisals for "disruptive activities" and began forcing them to drive on the right-hand side of the road.

If a Labour government had been in power in London, or even a Ted Heath sort of Conservative one, who knows but that the matter would have gone quickly to arbitration. Two factors prevented that. The first was that the *Sunday Times* had been leaked word of the invasion by someone in the British government, which in turn had seen CIA satellite photos of the Argentine preparations. The newspaper had its crack roving correspondent, Simon Winchester, on site to witness the striking of the Union Jack and the surrender of the governor, all of it recorded nicely on a single roll of film that he later had smuggled out to London—images which, when they appeared in newspapers round the world, forced Britain to retaliate. (Simon was later arrested as a spy, imprisoned, given a show trial, and sentenced to be executed by firing squad, which he probably would have been if the war hadn't ended in the nick of time.) The other factor was that Margaret Thatcher was of the ferocious old school and, what's more, was not without her own political difficulties at home that called for diversionary tactics. That Argentina didn't believe she would fight back doesn't speak well for its intelligence apparatus. A simple subscription to the *Daily Telegraph* probably would have been enough to let them foretell the future.

The British faced some considerable military obstacles in retaking the Falklands. The islands were twelve thousand eight hundred and eighty kilometres from the United Kingdom; the nearest British base, Ascension Island, in the mid-Atlantic, is about sixty-five hundred kilometres away. Their planes had to rely on two aircraft carriers saved from the scrapyard at the last minute, or else had to refuel in the air three times during each bombing run. (One pilot missed one of his refuelling rendezvous and made an emergency landing in Rio de Janeiro.) But then the British had fifteen to twenty nuclear submarines either in the South Atlantic or making for the area with all possible haste. They also had a fully professional army with a high proportion of elite forces such as the Gurkhas (at the sight of whom Argentines fled) and the Welsh Guards. Until troops could be brought in, British bombers cratered the airstrip at Port Stanley, the capital, keeping up such pressure that the facility had to be abandoned. Now there's a new and bigger British air base about forty kilometres outside town.

In the first phase the Falklands War was a naval contest. The United Kingdom declared an exclusionary zone of two hundred nautical miles round the islands, threatening to attack any ship that crossed it in an attempt to resupply or reinforce the Argentines on the ground. As it happened, the Argentine cruiser *Belgrado* was well outside the circle but was sunk anyway, as its intentions were clear. Nearly four hundred Argentines went down with it. One of the British tabloids, with the excess and poor taste for which the lower end of Fleet Street was renowned, ran a gigantic one-word headline on page one: GOTCHA! Two days later French-made Argentine jets from Tierra del Fuego fired an Exocet missile at HMS *Sheffield*, destroying it. Aluminum-hull construction was a new idea in ship-building at the time, poised to redirect the commercial shipping industry during the energy-crisis years by making everyone consider the use of these much lighter and more fuel-efficient vessels. The idea was killed off along with twenty sailors (another twenty were severely burned). When struck by an Exocet, it turned out, aluminum catches fire and melts, killing with lethal fumes. The *Sheffield* was replaced by HMS *Exeter*, a Type 42 destroyer equipped with Sea Harrier jump jets, which downed two of Argentina's Skyhawks and two of its Lear jets. But after the loss of the *Sheffield*, the Exocet was terrifying to the British, and with cause.

To supplement Royal Navy vessels, the British seconded two larger passenger liners, the *Canberra* and the *QE2,* to carry troops (three and a half thousand in the case of the *QE2* alone). Perfunctorily armed, they were easy marks for the Exocet-equipped jets. The loss of such a national symbol as the *QE2* and even a small portion of its human cargo might easily have cost Thatcher her government and her war. The French kindly lent Britain two of their Exocets as well as the engineers who had designed them so the British could study how best to avoid such a catastrophe. For their part the Americans continued to supply the British with satellite intelligence, and the flotilla arrived safely in stages.

The plan was to make an amphibious landing at Port San Carlos on the northwest corner of East Falkland, one of the two main islands, which are of approximately the same size. There was one spirited battle, with the British making a successful last-ditch assault on well-dug-in machine-gun positions near the town. But generally speaking the counterinvasion went smoothly for the British despite massed Argentine raids by as many as seventy aircraft. In all the British put about five thousand troops ashore and marched from San Carlos south and then east to Port Stanley. The British commander sent the following signal to London: "Please to inform Her Majesty that the Union Jack flies over Stanley once again." The British found themselves with an astounding sixteen thousand prisoners in their custody. They had to repatriate them to Argentina quickly before they starved or fell to disease. All told about eight hundred and ninety people on both sides had died, plus two civilian residents of the Falklands (nicknamed "kelpers") killed by a British bomb. Stanley was retaken on 14 June 1982. On 17 June, Argentines watched on television as General Galtieri resigned. Democratic elections in Argentina took place within twelve months. Cynics have sometimes wondered whether Thatcher would have gone to war if the handful of British subjects in the Falklands had been black, brown, or yellow rather than white.

Our own plan of attack on the Falklands was to strike first at a speck called West Point, off the northwest coast of West Falkland. To get there we would weave our way through many smaller pieces of rock, only one of which, the fetchingly named Carcus Island, was listed as inhabited. Dolphins swam alongside the ship, and the air overhead was filled with a few cormorants and a great number of large, graceful albatrosses. (Samuel Taylor Coleridge: "At length did cross an Albatross,/Thorough the fog it came;/As if it had been a Christian soul,/We hailed it in God's name.") We would anchor a kilometre and a half offshore and, weather permitting, effect an amphibious landing in zodiacs, those rigid inflatables designed by Jacques-Yves Cousteau. Orders called for us to hike a few kilometres over a rocky hill to visit a large rookery of two of the eighteen species of penguins, the chin-straps and the rock-hoppers. On the trek back we were to call at the house of the island's only inhabitants, a husband and wife who operated an Australian-style sheep station. But the weather didn't permit anything of the kind. We got to West Point all right. We were dressed in parkas and gloves, with all our warmest clothes underneath. Still, being on deck for more than a few minutes at a time was punishing.

Zodiacs, while ideal for scooting onto pebbly beaches, are also, because of their light weight, held in place mainly by the bums of the passengers, who sit on the pontoons, the air-filled modules of which the boats are made. A wind of twenty-five knots is considered the maximum for use of the zodiacs, and that would be a pretty wet ride. We arrived at our anchorage to find the wind gusting to fifty. After a certain amount of administrative humming and hawing, we raised the hook and set out round the top of the islands for Port Stanley on the opposite side of the colony, a trip estimated to take twelve hours but requiring twenty-four. We arrived offshore at 0600 and went in using a lifeboat as a tender.

The first Falklander I met, a young woman behind the counter at the tourist booth at the jetty where I'd stopped to pick up a street map, was an Argentine who didn't speak English and didn't know what I was talking about. But she was the only Argentine I saw in Stanley, though there must be many visitors from Buenos Aires and elsewhere to judge by the meticulous evenhandedness with which the late unpleasantness is handled in the charming little Port Stanley museum.

The town, which Sir Ernest Shackleton of all people said he found too desolate, houses about two-thirds of the twenty-five hundred civilians in the Falklands. It starts at the inner harbour and runs a half-dozen streets in depth. Visible behind the town is Tumbledown Mountain, where the Argentines made their last defence of the city. Except for the corrugated tin roofs and a few other oddities of style, Stanley looks remarkably like an English or Scottish village of a generation ago. Despite its supermarket and its Internet café, it is marked indelibly with the suggestion of being in a J. B. Priestley novel. It has a small Christ Church Cathedral, a row of brick terrace houses you'd swear were in Britain, the kind of red wooden phone boxes long obsolete in London, and a tiny police station whose size is in proportion to the crime problem. There is one bank, a Standard Chartered, and six public houses, one of which, the Victory Bar, advertises darts, pool, fruit machines, and "separate Ladies' & Gents' toilets." I can attest that this last claim is true. The facilities are in two unheated lean-tos appended to the outside back wall of the building.

Many of the structures are brightly painted red, blue, green, and when we arrived at the height of spring a few days before Christmas the front gardens were just as colourful, with well-cared-for plots of scotch broth, tulips, lupins—all sorts of flowers, native and otherwise. Behind some of the houses are sheds for storing peat, which many residents still use for fuel, though fewer and fewer in these good times when petrol is only thirty-six pence a litre and diesel is twenty-five pence. The well-paved and spotless streets are full of Land Rovers. Partly this is owed to the fact that before Liberation in 1982 there were no paved highways, which exist everywhere today; partly it's because the Land Rover, in Britain one of the most expensive personal vehicles, is in the Falklands one of the cheapest, due to favourable trade agreements and the fact that people pay virtually no taxes. Stanley has the usual number of village cranks, to judge from the two weekly newssheets, one of which is called the *Penguin Times*, but life is not stressful and the inner harbour insulates people against the worst outrages of winter. It speaks surprisingly well that young people who go away for postsecondary education nearly always return.

But make no mistake, this *is* a colony, er, overseas territory, with all the advantages and disadvantages for both parties. Eight local councillors serve as a legislature but can be vetoed (which doesn't happen often) by the governor from Britain appointed by the Foreign and Commonwealth Office for a three-year term. There is no independence movement in the Falklands. Nor is Britain eager to press independence on a place it repurchased with blood. As the inscription on the monument in Liberation Square reads: "In memory of those who liberated us 14 June 1982," a date whose anniversary is now a national holiday. Everything in Stanley is either "before 1982" or "after 1982." Before the war the islands were heavily subsidized by the mother country. Since the war, there has been a sizable military payroll. The exact number of troops is a secret, but there are some two thousand people in uniform at present, mostly Royal Air Force and Royal Navy personnel but with various ground units, from Gurkhas to Highlanders, rotating garrison duty. In recent years there have been as many as a thousand paratroopers in Stanley at one time. A navy vessel, HMS *Somerset*, is on permanent patrol round the islands.

Next to the bank in central Stanley is the ordnance office, where the bomb-disposal unit is based. Believing the British would begin their counteroffensive at Stanley, the Argentines laid enormous mine fields. The plastic antipersonnel devices, twice the size of hockey pucks, can't be located by metal detectors and aren't sensitive enough to be detonated by a sheep much less a penguin. But another variety is heat-sensitive—so much so that it can be set off by a human shadow falling over the spot where the mine lies. What's more, the mines decay and sometimes are victims of erosion, getting swept in and out with the tides. After the war, the army was issued with five robotic mine detonators on Cat-like treads. So far two of these vehicles have died in the service of their country, along with one unfortunate cow. Miraculously there have been no civilian mine casualties since war's end, mainly because the mine fields are so well delineated. There's one place in the Falklands where, in order to see the nesting penguins, birders must navigate a narrow catwalk, tip-toeing between the mine fields (story of my life). Many believe that the existing mine fields are being left intact in case "the Argies" ever reinvade. Mind you, I was able to purchase a detailed map of the fields for a pittance, and there's no reason to assume Argentines couldn't do the same. I chatted up the officer-in-charge as I bought my map. "We have downgraded the problem from a Danger to a Difficulty," he said with no irony whatsoever.

The town's modern twenty-eight-bed hospital is operated by the military but used by military and civilians alike. Many other facilities also owe their existence to the military presence. Floating docks erected in the inner harbour in 1982 are now used by smaller tour ships and supply vessels. By comparison, prefab eight-hundred-bed barracks called coastels were dismantled once the Liberation forces left. One is now a floating prison in New York City. There are, however, few direct subsidies from the British. This represents a wholesale change in policy from the time when the United Kingdom provided free houses. Such generosity is not needed nowadays. Once on its feet after the war, the Falklands asserted its territorial rights for a distance of two hundred nautical miles from the centre of the archipelago and began selling fishing rights to the fleets of other countries, especially South Korea and Spain. The Falklands are now the leading supplier of squid, and also a big source of fish such as red cod. Now comes renewed talk of oil exploration.

But Falkland Islanders have historically been clever at the task of making a living from such a bleakly beautiful but economically precarious landscape. At one time, before the opening of the Panama Canal in 1914, when many more ships sailed round the Horn of South America, battered vessels would put into Port Stanley for repairs. For years, in a kind of legalistic piracy, many ships that could have been saved were condemned as unseaworthy by the local admiralty court and sold at auction for less than their true value. A frequent purchaser was the Falkland Islands Company, the local monopoly. Other ships were wrecked near Stanley by storm or misadventure. The result is the Stanley Harbour Maritime History Trail, a well-marked walking tour where, within a few kilometres, one can see the hulks of several square-rigged wooden ships and many lesser vessels. Three of the less well-preserved wrecks are Canadian. The most important is the *Actaeon*, a five-hundred-and-sixty-one-tonne barque, built in New Brunswick in 1838, that came to rest at Stanley in 1853 after failing in an attempt to round the Horn.

Of the others, a few are the last of their breeds. The *Charles Cooper*, an American vessel said to be the best preserved of the seven thousand or so square-rigged merchant ships built in the United States, has been poking out of Stanley harbour since 1866. The

Jhelum, built in Liverpool in 1846, is something I never thought I'd see—an East Indiaman, or at least a ship in the manner of an East Indiaman, for the East India Company's charter had expired long before the vessel was built. Still, it is said to be the only one of its kind in the world still partly above water. Its bow is a bit stoved in, but the aft section, reflecting a design peculiar to such vessels, based on the East India Company's fleet, is quite well preserved, because that part of the hull was covered with corrugated iron when the hulk was used as a wool warehouse. The *Jhelum* was "condemned at Stanley" in 1870 when her crew, having taken a battering, refused to proceed to France.

The most dramatic and best preserved of the Stanley wrecks is the three-masted steel-clad barque *Lady Elizabeth*, which lies listing, all her masts and one spar intact, in Whalebone Cove on the north side of the inner harbour. It's a big ship of its type, one thousand two hundred and eight tonnes, and must have been a vessel of great majesty under full sail, for the empty shell, which we were able to get close to at low tide, is majestic even now. *Lady Elizabeth* foundered on a rock in the outer harbour in 1913, then, in the familiar pattern, was condemned and used as a floating warehouse until 1936 when a storm blew it sideways clear across the harbour to its present location, where it has slowly filled with sand. The *Lady Liz* is a favourite landmark for many Falkland Islanders. In 1982 a team of Britain's SAS commandos swam underwater from a submarine all the way across the outer harbour and then the inner one, using oxygen rebreathers rather than scuba gear, so as not to let bubbles give them away. They then penetrated the *Lady Liz*, making tunnels and caverns in the sand, where they took up long-term residence, monitoring all the military flights in and out of the original airfield, which lies only a few hundred metres away. The Argentines never caught on. Now, two decades later, this has become the worst-kept military secret of the Falklands War.

Back on the ship, lying in our own bunks, Bernadette and I imagined we could feel the moment when we crossed the Antarctic Convergence, the more or less circular imaginary line that surrounds the Antarctic ice mass and its assorted islands. We convinced ourselves we could tell by the sudden drop in temperature, the increase in roughness, and the decline in the ship's speed. We may have been reading too much into these feelings, but we did wake up early on the second morning out of the Falklands to find ourselves in the South Shetland Islands, off the top of the Antarctic Peninsula. Our destination was King George's Island. To be precise, Arcktowski, a small year-round Polish scientific station at 62°09s, 5829w, named after the Polish scientist Henryk Arcktowski. A number of nations have honoured their polar pioneers in this way. The old Soviet station was Bellingshausen after Admiral Thaddeus von Bellingshausen. Argentina's setup, Almirante Brown, was obviously called that after an admiral named Brown; its medical doctor, overcome by what one writer describes as "a spirit of burdensome exile," burned the place down in 1983 to force his country to evacuate him. The People's Republic of China named its site Great Wall Station. The British have shown the least imagination, christening theirs simply Base G.

Since 1971 when the Poles broke away from merely assisting in the Soviet Union's polar research and struck out on their own, between nineteen and twenty-five scientists and labourers have lived and worked at Arcktowski at one time in a cluster of prefabricated wooden or steel buildings that resemble the portables in Canadian elementary schoolyards. Our objective, however, was only partly the humanitarian one of providing a diversion for these lonely men, who stay at the base for a year or eighteen months before being rotated. Our primary one was to get as close as we could to the rookery of forty thousand gentoo penguins that live all bunched together on a snowy patch of glacier overlooking the stony, crescent-shaped shoreline.

The scientists study astronomy, cosmic rays, geomagnetic geology, seismology, and other topics. The penguins breed and occasionally waddle into the water to feed on krill, careful to avoid their natural predators, the fur seal and the elephant seal. The scientists busy themselves with their studies before retiring to the dormitories (some have lace-curtained windows), the mess hall, or the solar greenhouse. We found both species to be curious, inquisitive, and not at all frightened of visitors. The humans, to be sure, were positively grateful for our presence. Like, I suspect, most of the people at the sixty-eight scientific bases operated by seventeen countries in the Antarctic region, they see relatively few outsiders except those on the ships that supply them from home. But this is slowly changing as eco-tourism to the area becomes more popular. There are now enough tour companies taking people there that an organization, the International Association of Antarctic Tour Operators, has been formed and has helped establish the strict guidelines on human conduct (no walking on the lichens, for example). In fact, one of the most annoyingly frequent commercials on Australian television these days is for a charter airline that will fly you directly over the South Pole.

Admiralty Bay, where Arcktowski is located, was a site for whalers to camp. The beach stretches for perhaps three kilometres from a careened ship and a fuel storage tank at one end to a large rock at the other; on the lee side of the boulder various ships have attached plaques commemorating their visits and, in one case, a brass time capsule. This spot is littered with the bleached bones of whales, including jawbones four or four and a half metres in length. There are also rusty chains and other equipment used in the grisly rendering process, as well as an anchor—all of it just where it was left perhaps a hundred and twenty-five years ago. In the Arctic such material would have been put to other uses by the indigenous inhabitants, but Antarctica, of course, has none. On a similar beach on South Georgia Island, considerably north the South Shetlands, there is still a huge cauldron from the same era.

When the penguins leave the rookery, they walk in pairs, like nuns in black-and-white habits. For this was mating season. Sometimes they flap their wings or bury their heads in their chests or else throw back their beaks and perform a pantomime of gargling. When seen en masse, though, the effect of penguins is more like that of a moneyed crowd in formal dress. Intermission at the Royal Opera House perhaps.

As on a ship, rigid class distinctions are observed in the camp. The highly educated scientists don't have much to do with the working-class truck drivers or heavy-equipment operators. And unfortunately we couldn't either, because while most of the former speak English, the latter have only Polish. Sighting us coming, a geophysicist in his late forties (he looked a bit like Allen Ginsberg in his late only-slightly-bearded period) rushed out and waited for us to splash ashore in our rubber wellies. "Please, what is the name of your vessel? Can you tell me this? You see, I am writing a letter home and wish to include the news of your arrival." We happily told him and he brought out some chairs for us to sit on. It turned out that as a courtesy we would take his and everybody else's letters with us when we went at the end of the day, for later mailing at the next place with a post office. We also brought them gifts: beer and fresh fruit, including a watermelon, which looked faintly ridiculous in Antarctic surroundings. The beer, they said, would go down especially well in front of the television, where they watch cassettes of Hollywood and Polish films, the same ones again and again. In return they sold us T-shirts with their logo on them.

Our visit in December coincided with the Antarctic summer. Sunrise was at 0258 hours, sunset at 2259. When we upped anchor at the end of the day and pushed on southwest towards Deception Island, the evening sunlight glittered on the icebergs, which sometimes have huge blue seams running through them: the same blue as Windex. The house-size pieces that have broken off are called bergie bits. They were plentiful. So were the tiny (grand-piano-size) ones called growlers. On the way to Deception these formations sometimes seemed alarmingly close to the ship.

An overnight sail took us past another scientific station, which was being serviced by a three-masted schooner. My binoculars weren't strong enough to make out its flag for certain, but I believe it was Argentine.

Deception itself, uninhabited by humans, is an interesting place in a number of ways. It was there that the first American to see the Antarctic mainland did so, catching a glimpse of the long Antarctic Peninsula. This was also the scene of the first manned flight in Antarctica, when an Australian pilot took to the air, a short time before Admiral Richard Byrd's more famous venture. What's more, Deception is both a glacier and an active volcano. Parts of the glacier are black from volcanic sand and ash embedded in the ice fields.

The morning—Christmas morning, as it happened—was one of calm seas, so the zodiacs were lowered. Our intention was to enter the narrow, almost clandestine passage that's thought to give Deception its name. Beyond this doorway lay a caldera where the volcanic mountain collapsed aeons ago, creating a crater lake with a water temperature of about sixteen degrees Celsius. But though the short trip to the entrance was successful, we couldn't cross the threshold, as there was so much ice bobbing round just outside the warm zone that we feared we would damage the propellers of the Yamaha 40s that powered the boats. So we enjoyed short rides between the ship and the scene of our disappointment, returning for a traditional English Christmas dinner. We had all been up since 0530 or so and therefore made an early night of it. We spent Boxing Day securing everything in our cabin for what was expected to be that night's rough crossing of the Drake Passage. As we worked, we kept putting on and peeling off layers of clothes, as the cabin had turned cold on us for the first time. "I am not seasick, dammit," Bernadette would say defiantly, pausing occasionally to vomit.

We were headed for Ushuaia in the Argentine part of Tierra del

Fuego, which, situated as it is on the Beagle Channel, lays claim to being the world's southernmost city. Certainly it isn't among the most compelling, though it's not without a frontier appeal, with many log buildings and the bustle that one expects wherever people are hoping to earn a big bankroll in a short period of time. For some, *Ushuaia* is known only as the title of an adventure travel series on cable television. I guess I can understand why. The place reminded me of Whitehorse at the opposite end of the world.

GOING TO HELL BY SEA

$\mathcal{W}$e went ashore in Chile and made our way to Santiago where I wrangled an east-facing room at the stately Hotel Carerra, a splendid place of medium size built in 1940 but suggestive of 1920, what with its marble, rare hardwoods, and general air of craftsmanship in every architectural and design detail. Like many other grand hotels in Latin America (Asia too), the Carrera serves unofficially as a permanent gallery of its country's finest visual art. Ignoring the hard-to-ignore mosaics in the fore-lobby, depicting the pageant of Chilean history, you proceed upstairs to find that the guest floors hold a discriminating private collection of the most striking contemporary Chilean painting.

The Carrera is a preserve of old-fashioned service as well. Everything is quiet, very discreet, but not sepulchral. You never know the security personnel are security personnel until you see them spot one of the city's innumerable pickpockets and cutpurses trying to enter the building by the ruse of being dressed up. The potential miscreants are escorted out in a firmly but what seems to the casual onlooker a friendly enough fashion, as though some muscular fellows were taking them to lunch. Male and female security people, dressed as something else, sit all night behind unmarked doors on each guest floor. Patrons never see them, never even guess they're there, but jewel thieves fear them. That's the way it's supposed to be.

Our window overlooked the Plaza de la Constitución, with the big international banks and the offices of *La Nación* to the left, the Justice ministry and the snow-dipped Andes straight ahead, and the president's office to the right. The last of these is called La Moneda because, until 1958, it also served as the country's mint. This dual role was a great convenience for fleeing despots who were able to load up on gold coins before embarking on new careers in exile. This was the building in which President Salvador Allende died: a suicide or an assassination victim, depending on whom you listen to. In fact, La Moneda was almost totally destroyed in the coup on 11 September 1973, which resulted in the military regime led by General Pinochet. It's long since been fully, faithfully, and beautifully rebuilt and restored inside and out. As a reminder of history, however, some bullet damage has been permitted to remain on a government office building adjoining the Carrera on the north. A tour of La Moneda requires ten days' notice. The Carrera, however, is the perfect vantage point from which to watch the changing-of-the-guard ceremony outside La Moneda's gates far below. It's an impressive sight, involving cavalry as well as foot soldiers and even that rarity, a military band worth hearing. To save money the guard is changed only on alternating days. By comparison the bed linen at the Carrera is changed twice daily whether anyone has used it or not. Of course, this is done in such a way that the guests are expected not to notice. The Carrera is never officious. Also, it is not without its own colourful history—not simply of famous guests who have stayed there (all old upper-end hotels can make that boast), but rather of history that has unfolded there.

In 1985 pro-democracy guerrillas took one of the most desirable rooms in the hotel, smuggled in a shoulder-fired rocket launcher in pieces, and attempted to blow up Pinochet's office. The backblast set the room on fire, destroying it and damaging others. Tsk-tsk. In a very short time the hotel's management made certain no trace of the incident remained. But everyone realized its importance; the episode was the beginning of the end for Pinochet, though the junta lasted another five years. Perhaps the dressiest party in Chile on the millennial New Year's Eve took place around the pool atop the hotel, where women in tiaras (really) watched what was probably the world's biggest fireworks display that night—far longer and more spectacular than London's, for example. The hotel was the perfect base for a few days, except that Bernadette was ricocheting off the costly wall coverings without her antidepressants. One night, to get some peace, I had to sleep curled up like a dog on a small sofa, misnamed a love seat in this case. Yet we had a reasonably peaceful coexistence, because the city offered much to explore, and I learned she was at her best when we kept moving.

What we first discovered in our wanderings is that, like most of the other South American capitals, Santiago is a city of gracious parks, impressive boulevards, and stinking slums. Like most of the others, and presumably in imitation of Rio, it has a huge religious statue, visible for miles, atop one of its highest mountains—in this case, the Virgin on a peak named Cerra San Cristóbal. When you take the funicular up the summit of San Cristóbal—again like the other important cities, Santiago is rich in funiculars, though not to the extent that Valparaíso is—you find little shops selling bronze-coloured tin plaques of Chile's heroes: Jesus Christ, Salvador Allende, Che Guevara, and Pablo Neruda. In addition there's a little stall that sells, for only a few pesos each, copies of miniature editions of a couple of Neruda's works. The books are about the size of large commemorative postage stamps and as brightly coloured; they're obviously intended for the common audience. This touched me somehow.

At the bottom of San Cristóbal, in the Bellavista district, is one of Neruda's houses, La Chascona, a two-storey affair, fieldstone on the bottom and bright blue wood above, built right into the hillside. The poet commenced work on it in the early 1950s with the last of his trinity of wives, Matilde Urrutia, after whom it is named ("La Chascona" translates more or less as "the Tangled One," a reference to her hard-to-manage hair). They met in 1946 but didn't move in together until 1955, once he had separated from Delia del Carril. Pepe Donoso's novel *Toque de queda* is set during Urrutia's funeral, a time of great public mourning. Theirs is one of the great literary love stories.

The house, located on a steep cul-de-sac, hard to find without good intuition or a trained guide, is actually a collection of smaller buildings within a multilevel compound. This is fitting because Neruda was a collector of everything from butterflies to signed photographs to glass paperweights. Therefore he was also a collector of houses in which to display them. There is a second Neruda home in Valparaíso and a third in the seaside village of Isla Negra, all of them administered by the Neruda Fundación. La Chascona gives some sense of what Urrutia was like. It reveals her interest in the cutting-edge art of the 1960s, for example. You also get some sense of Delia del Carril, a painter, a generation younger than Neruda, whom he met in 1934 but left in 1955. The sense comes from two of Carril's canvases displayed there. All three houses show Neruda's whimsical taste in architecture, even though the second house, in Valparaíso, was one he bought rather than had built. It's called La Sebastiana and is next door to what looks like the art deco theatre it once was but is now a dog-food factory.

Valparaíso, which Neruda once wrote of as "a filthy rose," sprawls on the Pacific, an hour's drive or more from Santiago, depending on the time of day and the time of year. It functions as Santiago's port city. Its great boom days were during the California gold rush when so many ships stopped there after coming round the Horn, but the opening of the Panama Canal in 1914 seemed to doom it. The harbour silted over more than once. As a result, the city is still rich in old architecture, which was probably as much of an attraction for Neruda as the sea itself. In recent years the city has become more important, largely because the Congress was moved there when democracy was restored to the country in 1990: an odd case of the legislature not being in the capital. As usual Neruda made unusual use of interior space and plastered La Sabastiana with the work of artisan friends, mosaicists especially in this case. The British travel writer Sara Wheeler, on whose information I rely for some of this detail, remarks that the house is tall and thin, like the country.

Far and away the most famous and popular of Neruda's houses is the one at Isla Negra, a fantastical place built atop a huge beach boulder a short distance south of Valparaíso. When, at fifty-nine, Neruda wrote his autobiography in verse (his prose one appeared posthumously eleven years later), he called it *Memorial de Isla Negra*, so thoroughly had he become associated with the place, so essential had the house become to him. The day Bernadette and I drove there from Santiago was hot but the traffic light, so the trip took only an hour. Neruda and Urrutia are buried there side by side, facing the pounding Pacific surf.

Ordinary South Americans love their famous contemporary writers in a way that has no counterpart in North America. Such figures as Jorge Amado in Brazil and Gabriel García Márquez in Colombia have a spot in the people's hearts and affections that is difficult for Canadian or American writers not to envy. An ad I saw for a bed-and-breakfast in the *Buenos Aires Herald* listed its main attribute as "Located in Borges' Neighbourhood."

Although at least two hundred books by and about Neruda and his poetry have been written in English, no adequate English-language biography exists: a puzzling state of affairs for one so popular and acclaimed. Those of us without sufficient Spanish to read any of the half-dozen Spanish-language biographies are left to grope about for the facts of his life. In Chile, however, virtually everyone knows the sad story of the happy and somewhat childlike Pablo. He was born in 1904 in Parral, three hundred or so kilometres south of Santiago, but reared in Temuco, a frontier town, where Gabriela Mistral, Chile's other Nobel Prize–winning poet, was headmistress of a

Catholic girls' school. Mistral (the nom de plume of Lucila Godoy de Alcayaga) lent him courage and also the works of Feodor Dostoyevsky and others. At twelve Neruda was translating Charles Baudelaire, at fourteen publishing his first poems in literary journals. He removed to Santiago in 1921, ostensibly to get his credentials as a teacher of French but also to live the literary and bohemian life in an area centred on a street called Londres-Paris (near the Church of San Francisco, the only such building in Santiago to survive the great earthquake of 1664). At this stage Neftalí Ricardo Reyes Basoalto began taking the name Pablo Neruda, borrowing from the Czech writer Jan Neruda. In 1923 an anarchist group published *Crepusculario*, his first collection of poetry. In 1924 came his most famous one, *Viente poemas de amor*, which appeared initially in an edition of five hundred copies and would go on to sell over two million; it remains a favourite book for men to give to their beloved. In between times he went to Paris and met Pablo Picasso: the first indication of how peripatetic his life would be, not always pleasantly so.

Like many other poets and writers, he found himself in the diplomatic service, serving in minor posts in Burma, Ceylon, and Java, then in Buenos Aires, Barcelona, and Madrid. The last two postings coincided with the Spanish Civil War when he became a communist and saved the lives of many writers, artists, and musicians by spiriting them out of the country. His return to Chile unhappily coincided with the election of Francisco Franco's fellow fascist González Videla, which drove Neruda into exile in Mexico—on horseback. He returned and left again according to the political climate. At its most favourable he was made a senator, in 1945, though the supreme court later expelled him from the chamber because he was a communist. In 1938, before beginning this cycle of exile, he was also on horseback when he stumbled on a one-room cabin overlooking the sea at Isla Negra. The owner was one of the Spaniards whom Neruda had saved, and a deal was struck, though Neruda didn't return to the site until 1952. This cabin became the dining room of Neruda's eccentric house, which seems to have spread in all directions, one room at a time, as finances allowed.

Much of it is built to resemble a ship, with rounded wooden ceilings, narrow companionways, and hemp rope on the walls, while other, later parts are made of rough logs to remind him of the Temuco of his childhood. Neruda loved the sea—his writing desk was a hatch cover from a sailing ship that had come ashore as drift-wood—but was afraid of the water. Someone gave him an old fishing boat, which he installed in his garden. He and his guests (the house was a magnet for the famously talented) would climb into it for cocktails before lunch. Nearby is a tall A-shaped frame made of logs; ships' bells hang from every level. Eventually the home on Isla Negra expanded to sixty-nine thousand seven hundred and fifty square metres to house all his collections. The library he kept there has been donated to a university, along with a collection of six thou-sand seashells, so that the house is less full of his literary personality than one might wish. But the severity of his collecting mania—no other term will do—is evident. Neruda collected music instruments, though he played none. He collected ships' figureheads, including one he bought from the surrealist writer and visual artist Ludwig Zeller when Zeller was fleeing Chile for Canada. These take up one entire room. Another is given over to his ships-in-bottles. Wine, pipes, scrimshaw, stamps, erotic French postcards, plumbing fixtures, and stirrups were other interests. Coloured glass bottles, of which he had thousands, held such special significance for him that he wouldn't drink anything, even water, from a clear glass. But then colour in general was an important part of his life. He wrote only in green ink, in his writing room, built in the 1960s, surrounded by likenesses of the writers he most admired: Edgar Allan Poe, Joseph Conrad, Charles Baudelaire, John Keats, Victor Hugo, and especially Walt Whitman (figures, some of them, whose pictures also hang at the Santiago house).

When he was in exile, the Chilean government kept trying to

extradite him to stand trial for being a communist, which had become a crime ex post facto. In the 1950s, when he was safely returned, his political confidence grew to the point where, by the late 1960s, he decided to run for president as the Communist Party candidate. In the end, to avoid splitting the left-wing vote, he stepped aside in favour of his old friend Salvador Allende, a socialist who had already sought the post more than once. This decision swung the communist vote to Allende, who won. In gratitude Allende appointed Neruda ambassador to France.

Neruda was awarded the Nobel Prize for literature in 1971. The tuxedo he wore to the ceremony (his smoking suit as Europeans used to say—he refers to it in a poem as *"el smoking"*) hangs in the closet at Isla Negra. So does the cap and gown he wore to receive his honorary D.Litt. from Oxford. Not that all his honours came from the West: he was also a recipient of the prestigious Lenin Prize from the Soviet Union. Sadly he was already ill with prostate cancer when he learned of the Nobel Prize. But he was sick with something else as well. Chile was sick. Allende's social programmes, such as the traditional Latin American one of land redistribution, frightened capitalist governments everywhere, particularly the United States, which was further outraged by the nationalization of Chile's biggest industry at the time, its copper mines. The Nixon White House and the CIA were out to get Allende, whose policies heightened justice but proved disastrous for the economy. In 1973 unemployment peaked at thirty-seven percent; inflation was a thousand percent (having fallen from five thousand). On 11 September 1973, Allende died of a gunshot wound. According to the latest information, revealed in an interview by his daughter Isabel Allende (not to be confused with his niece of the same name, the novelist who lives in San Francisco), he killed himself with a pistol given him as a gift by Fidel Castro. But as one *chileano* said to me, "Of course, there's no way of knowing who it was who said, 'Here's Castro's gun. You have fifteen minutes,' and then waited behind the chair."

On that same day Pablo Neruda died of cancer—or a broken heart—after hearing the news on the radio. Augusto Pinochet, a relatively obscure career officer from the north, then led the country on a bloody reign of terror and torture that killed many thousands, exiled many thousands more, and restored the faith of investors. Neruda's body was transferred from Isla Negra ("Little Sur," Bernadette called it) to La Chascona in Santiago which, like the other houses, had been ransacked and vandalized by Pinochet's troops. His wake was held amid broken glass.

As I write this, Pinochet is in exile, having avoided trial for crimes against humanity. Superficially Chile is prosperous and peaceful. In Santiago the visitor will occasionally stumble on a *zona restringida*, but then there is the occasional *zona de picnic* to offset the feeling. As elsewhere, Bernadette and I saw accumulating evidence of economic polarization and the vise grip in which the middle classes are being squeezed until they pop. Within a block of Carrera and wherever we went using public and private transport, both in Santiago and in outlying towns and villages, the signs were familiar. A sweater in a shop window, instead of bearing a price tag, had a sign indicating the amount of each of fourteen installment payments; everyone in Chile seems to smoke cigarettes (Bernadette was in nicotine addicts' heaven) but finding smokes by the carton is difficult, because most people can afford to buy only a pack at a time or even a few individual cigarettes. As for the other end of Santiago's economy, we saw it in abundance the night of the *fiesta milenio* when the twentieth century gave way to the twenty-first; socially speaking, this was the biggest evening of seismic activity since the 1985 earthquake, 7.6 on the Richter scale.

We had driven back to Santiago by a different route, going through the farming communities of Melipilla and Pomaire. The latter is a village destroyed in the same quake and since taken over by potters and other artisans, where one of the shops sells clay busts of "P. Neruda." We got back in time to bag dinner before all eating places closed for the festivities. We chose the kind of all-you-can-eat buffet known as a *tenedor libre* (free fork). The hotel had hired the Plaza de la Constitución for the evening, for the use of guests and especially the Santiago elite who came in tuxedos and lavish gowns, the women trailing jewels. As servants are given the night off on New Year's Eve, they brought their children, hundreds of them in all, whom the hotel had made arrangements to entertain and to nanny.

That morning we had looked down and seen the changing-of-the-guard ceremony in front of the presidential palace, but now the same area was populated with soldiers in fatigues, erecting metal barricades to close off the plaza to traffic and riffraff. The much less scary civil police were patrolling the area with a studied and practised casualness. A peculiarity of the civil police in Chile is that although there are many female officers on the beat, they seem less equal than female officers in other places. They wear stylish uniforms and are taught makeup and poise in addition to the usual police arts. Their small gold-coloured earrings are standard issue, part of their uniform, just like the holsters, which that night, I noticed, were empty—unlike those of their male colleagues, who carried the usual nine-millimetre Glock automatics beloved of cops worldwide. Was this because someone feared the women might be overpowered and mugged for their weapons?

One block away a huge lighted stage had been erected and a celebrity concert by Chile's leading rock stars was getting under way. Video cams on agile booms a couple of storeys above the ground recorded the whole event, including the pause to announce the winning lottery numbers, for simultaneous projection on an enormous digital screen for the hundreds of thousands of ordinary citizens who had jammed into the area from the Avenida de

Liberados Bernardo O'Higgins. (The street is named after the revolutionary who freed Chile from Spain. His real name was simply Higgins. Like Daniel Foe and Thomas Quincey, he thought it needed some orthographic embellishment.)

A laser show turned the scene of Allende's death and Pinochet's rule first emerald, then madder rose. The sky was pissing confetti. Vendors were barely able to make their way between the shoulders of the people—atop which sat many a small child (including a two-year-old boy in a tiny tux) who, their parents hoped, would always remember being present at the death of the old millennium and the birth of the new. Two huge electrical clocks, one beside the stage, the other atop a telecom tower (a local landmark), counted down the minutes and seconds to the new year and the fresh century. The clocks, however, weren't quite in agreement. Bernadette and I, holding hands lest we get separated and subsumed into the crowd, never to be reunited, left just as the expectation was becoming almost unbearable and nipped round the corner back to the Plaza de la Constitución. Our Carrera room key was enough to persuade the troops to let us through the barriers. We weren't wearing fancy dress, but we had the obvious look of a gringa and her gringo.

On the grassy square in front of the hotel and the palace, we sat on the ground and watched the thirty-seven-minute display of fireworks, the finest I have ever witnessed live or on film, that began at the telecom tower as soon as the first two digits of the incoming age flashed on the digital clock face. Somehow we avoided being trampled underfoot by the still formally dressed but now already drunken members of the social elite who had left the hotel to watch from their own private area, oblivious to their less fortunate countrymen a hundred metres away. When the display was over, the wealthy began to pass back to the hotel, where they had already made quite a mess, I learned later. I wondered how many people present, hearing the explosions that seemed to shake the sky, recalled the storming of the palace twenty-seven years earlier. I had no way to know anyone's private thoughts. When the last smoke streamers evaporated in the night sky and the crowd had thinned considerably, a small fire somehow started in a pile of discarded banners and placards in the dead centre of the park. A young soldier hurried over and stomped it out with his big paratrooper boots before it could ignite the dry grass. And then it was dark. Bernadette and I had a glass of Chilean champagne in our room, ate cold chicken we had wisely laid by, and then went to bed. Because my flailing about on the unexpectedly soft and luxuriant mattress had disturbed her sleep on the penultimate night of the twentieth century, I took a pillow and the coverlet back to the overstuffed little semicircular sofa that was about half as long am I am tall. My feeling was not: Where did the twentieth century go so quickly? My question was: Is it really *only* 2000?

Bernadette and I were a volatile mix at the best of times, and she announced she had decided to stay on in Santiago (her Spanish is excellent) while I caught a plane back to Ushuaia, where the ship now was. We would rendezvous when the vessel reached Easter Island in nine or ten days' time. I wondered whether she would actually show up. No, I was sure I'd be seeing her again, because I remembered that she had left her biggest and heaviest suitcase in our cabin. I liked everything about her except her temper, which I presumed, hopefully, was merely an expression of her not having her medication with her.

Ushuaia was cold but clear when I got there, and I had more of a chance to assess the site and talk to people. I learned again that everything is indeed reversed when you go from the northern hemisphere to the southern. For example, Chileans travel south to Ushuaia in the same way Americans head north to Alaska, to make big money for a while on the frontier. But they are people without roots in the community which, accordingly, has the not-well-looked-after appearance of a transient camp, though it has as many people as there are taxis in Santiago, about forty-five thousand. Nor is the infrastructure more than basic; the town gets its water supply from a small glacier. Links with the past can be fragile. Only six months earlier a fifty-six-year-old woman named Virginia Choinquitel died of a heart attack, the last of the full-blooded Ona people whose history in Tierra del Fuego extended back nine thousand years and who were once hunted by professionals for a bounty. To collect the bounty the hunters needed to turn in only one ear for each kill.

Chile hasn't always got on well with its neighbours. More than a century after the close of the Pacific War in which it expanded its territory greatly, Chile still hasn't fully restored diplomatic relations with Bolivia, its co-opponent on that occasion (along with Peru). Tierra del Fuego, which is cut in two geographically by the various passages that are the tortuous alternatives to sailing round the Horn, is cut off politically as well, by the border dividing Chile from Argentina. In recent decades there has sometimes been considerable tension about the boundary. As a result, the Argentine government in Buenos Aires, well over a thousand kilometres to the north, has made a deliberate point of building up the population of its half of Tierra del Fuego. It has done so by locating there the factories where electronic products and household appliances are assembled. Hence the boom.

The main Chilean community is Porvenir at the north end, but the rival to Ushuaia is Punta Arenas. Chileans claim *this* is the world's most southerly city, being more than twice the size of Ushuaia, which the Chileans dismiss as a mere town. The argument is mainly semantic, for Ushuaia is on the fifty-fourth parallel and Punta Arenas on the fifty-third. The pleasure in being able to see them both is not to compare and contrast but rather to make the passage through the northern arm of the Beagle Channel to the Strait of Magellan on which Punta Arenas (sandy point indeed) is located. The trip is slow and somewhat hazardous. Precipitation is more or less constant so that cataracts tumble down the sides of the Chilean fjords and there is always a rumour of menace in the air. At certain places glaciers run right down to the end of the channel, which can be quite narrow. This is the seagoing equivalent of wandering through a maze of deep canyons. By seeming to feel our way, we turned up the next morning at Punta Arenas, a place of three thousand millimetres of rain a year and home to Magellan penguins almost beyond number and six kinds of whale, including the blue, the largest mammal in the world. This part of the trip took place on the forty-sixth day of the voyage.

Tierra del Fuego has traditionally been used as a penal colony as well as a place of opportunity. Only a few days before our visit Argentina sentenced Lino Cesar Oviedo, an exiled Paraguayan general, to confinement there for breaking the terms of his residence by granting a newspaper an interview about politics. In fact, prisoners made up part of Fort Bulnes, which the Chileans built in 1843 at the urging of Bernardo O'Higgins. The stronghold turned out to be a dreadful failure in terms of weather, potable water, and the resistance, which had been underestimated, of the local aboriginals (of whom about seven thousand remained as late as 1880). But the arrival of the governor and his garrison was enough to thwart the ambitions of the French, who only a short time earlier had accepted the Chileans' invitation to "retire the flag." What finally brought down Fort Bulnes was a mutiny, during which the governor was executed by being tied to the mouth of a cannon that was then discharged. The place was abandoned in 1848 and the settlement moved forty kilometres north—the present Punta Arenas. In 1946 the fort was reconstructed on its original site. The reconstruction looks about as convincing as such attempts usually do, though care was taken to build as the garrison had been made, with houses fashioned from peat surrounded by a log palisade. The location is of interest, rather, for its beautiful isolation. A few hundred metres farther down the trail lies the southernmost point in mainland Chile, the spot where Ferdinand Magellan found the alternative route to the Pacific, which you can actually see off to the southwest, among an assortment of islands, beyond which lies nothing but a portion of Antarctica claimed by Chile, an assertion disputed hotly by others.

The sea round Punta Arenas is lined with fishing boats—the commonest size is eleven metres—which go out every morning for hake, cod, king crab, and sea urchins. As for the shore, it doesn't seem odd somehow to find sheep in a place where penguins also live, as in the Falklands. The early robber barons of Punta Arenas, some of whose mansions are still to be seen in the town, made their fortunes in wool. Fire bush and Magellan oak are common. So are fields of daisies. So is wind, which is often too strong to permit football games. Flamingos are found there, too, as are skunks and pesky squirrels, which were introduced from abroad and are now a plague to subsistence farmers. Every now and then there is a report of someone being injured by a puma.

Punta Arenas is right to call itself a city whereas Ushuaia is merely a town. Punta Arenas has a cathedral, a department store, and all the other amenities, sacred and secular, that define cities. It also has the problems. The port, Catalina, next to the airport, is less than five kilometres from the Plaza Munoz Gamero, the main square. During that short trip, you pass from a struggling industrial zone to prosperous new suburbs to a central area that is plainly dying, with vacant commercial property and a general absence of charm. And an abundance of police and military, as elsewhere in Chile. Yet the navy gave us hospitality of a kind. As a breakwater for the naval yard, three old ships have been scuttled. You walk through the rusting hulls of the first two to arrive at the third, a square-rigged merchant ship, the *County of Peebles*, built on the Clyde in the 1870s; its original poop is now a club for officers. The other point that struck me was how even down there the merchants still practise the siesta, closing the shops from 1200 to 1500, as though this were a tropical place, not the frigid bottom of the world where people wear heavy windbreakers and even parkas at the zenith of summer. This shows the thoroughness with which the Spanish colonized and also how culture is stronger than logic.

Such was the image I carried in my head when, after the usual unexplained delays, we set sail that night for Easter Island, a passage of nine days' duration, during which the weather began to warm again as the ship broke out of the Humboldt Extension, the cold current that hugs the Pacific coast of South America. As the Chileans say, "Cold water, good seafood." We spent one night in a gale amid the customary shattered glassware. Just as the southern hemisphere is a mirror of the northern, so the currents are to the subsea world as the winds are to the one above: they both move round with the seasons. And we had both factors going against us. As so often in the past, I stopped to shake my head at what the days of sail must have been like. As it was, I awoke every quarter hour or so through most of the night whenever a big shiver seemed to pass aft to forward through the hull plates. These tremors were caused by the props spinning madly when not underwater where they were supposed to be.

When we arrived at Easter Island just before dawn one morning, I came face-to-face with one of the ghosts of my childhood. I refer to Thor Heyerdahl, the Norwegian—what? explorer? adventurer?—whose book *The Kon-Tiki Expedition* (Oslo 1948, London 1950) was a work all boys my age read in the late 1950s. We didn't know this at the time, but the book was the foundation of an entire school of crank exploration in which people undertake silly voyages in order to prove the Vikings discovered the source of the Mississippi or Marco Polo visited California. It is a genre whose respectable face is represented by Tim Severin, but one that also included the Swiss crackpot Erich von Daniken, who believed that the famous stone images of Easter Island were erected by extraterrestrials (von Daniken saw extraterrestrials everywhere). In fact, respectable scientific investigation long ago robbed the Easter Island story of most of its mystery, leaving only the beauty of the place.

The island now called Easter was so named by the Dutch explorer Jacob Roggeveen, who sighted it on Easter Sunday 1722, but it has had many other names. Whatever it's called, it's a little pip of a place one hundred and sixty-eight square kilometres in size and shaped like a boomerang, with extinct volcanoes at each corner. The tallest of them is five hundred and seven metres, and from the tip of it one can see the ocean three hundred and sixty degrees and take comfort (or not) in being in what many consider the most isolated permanently inhabited spot on Earth, three thousand seven hundred and forty kilometres from the nearest part of South America. But is it isolated enough? That's the question. About twenty-seven hundred people, twenty-five percent of them Chileans, live on Rapa Nui, as the place is known in the local language. All of them are somehow connected with tourism. The modern airport is the culprit. Easter Island is part of Chile (to be precise, part of District 12, administered from Valparaíso), and the state airline, LanChile, brings *turistas* in an unending stream to see the famous stone heads (*moai*) and the stone platforms (*ahu*) on which they're erected, even though all the upright effigies have been righted only in the past century and aren't necessarily on their original sites. The airport is big enough to accommodate the Concorde, which used to arrive about three times a year. Hotels, guest houses, and souvenir shops make up the better part of Hanga Roa, the only town.

At one time over two thousand moai stood, facing the sea. The tallest is about ten metres and weighs seventy-three thousand kilograms. Nearly all were quarried and carved at one site, about six kilometres from the closest destination. Another seven hundred or so, the biggest about twenty metres and two hundred and forty-five thousand kilograms, were abandoned in various quarries in one stage of completion or another. The effigies don't have Polynesian features, but serious researchers always have known that the island culture that produced these statues, and then suddenly stopped doing so, was part of the great eastward migration of Polynesian sailors that settled places as far apart as Fiji, Tahiti, the Marquesas, New Zealand, and Hawaii. Heyerdahl's contention was that Easter Islanders came west from South America, where they had learned their engineering skills from contact with the first Europeans there. To prove that this was feasible he sailed a balsa raft, only 5.4 by 3.6 metres, from Peru to Raroia in Polynesia, proving nothing very much except that rafts can float but becoming a major bestselling celebrity in the process—and provoking a rash of other writings about the island, about which there was already a considerable body of work.

Take, for example, John Macmillan Brown's 1924 book *The Riddle of the Pacific*, in its way one of the key works in the field, one thought for so long to be famously mysterious. The riddle of Brown's title is, of course, the familiar one of who the original inhabitants were—ancient Polynesians moving from the west to the east or an aboriginal group sailing west from South America? Stylistically there is at least some evidence for both, though the two viewpoints are by no means equal in plausibility. The consensus, however, has never been unclear. There has also always been a hidden note of racism in the supposedly new theories. Consider the Adena and related Early Woodland cultures that existed in North America two thousand years ago, from what is now southern Ontario all the way down the Ohio and Mississippi valleys. What's left today to recall their existence is the series of variously shaped mounds all along this corridor. The people who built them had long since disappeared before the arrival of the Europeans. The white newcomers were unwilling to believe that the ancestors of the "Indians" they saw round them could possibly have had such engineering skills. Hence the many tracts and commentaries speculating that the mounds must have been built by the Lost Tribes of Israel, to whom all such mysteries were attributed until secular cold war times when extra-terrestrials took over as the stock answer.

The moai were quarried from volcanic stone on the island (some half-finished ones can be seen still attached to the face of the quarrying site). Until modern times, however, there was a similar "mystery" about how such primitive people could move pieces weighing many tonnes, though in fact the question is easily answered. They first cut them free from the mother stone, padded the moai bellies to protect them, and then pushed them along a bit at a time using a line suspended from a bipod, which they repositioned every metre or so. By the same method, they hoisted the moai onto the already-prepared ahu, which are far more numerous than the complete moai and must have been used for more than one purpose. Argument about who did such work is divided into books written before and after Heyerdahl, who began in Peru and sailed eight thousand kilometres in the kind of boat the Mayans made and who then, in a later book, *Aku-Aku*, showed how the moai could have been erected.

The first private archaeological expedition, in 1914, resulted in Katherine Routledge's 1919 book *The Mystery of Easter Island: The Story of an Expedition*. But Brown's more popular 1924 work has the most detail about the island. Many of his assumptions haven't been taken up by others. For example, he insisted that all the ahu were burial platforms. But he was the first to see the island's present inhabitants as descendants of the people who built the moai. Most of the works subsequent to his have been reports with specific purposes, such as Alfred Metraux's *Ethnology of Easter Island*, based on fieldwork undertaken in the 1930s. But some, such as *Island at the Centre of the World* (1970) by Sebastian Englert, a German priest who lived on Rapa Nui for thirty-five years, are unsponsored, independent scholarship. Students of Easter Island have always included these private sector as well as public-sector inquirers, though most have been tied to expeditions of various kinds, whether Chilean, American, European, or even Canadian. The Canadian contribution to the literature is *World Away: A Canadian Adventure on Easter Island* by Helen Evans Reid (1965), an account of an expedition by a

Canadian medical and scientific group that left Halifax aboard HMCS *Cape Scott* to study Easter Island's environment—a worthy initiative far ahead of its time. There are also a number of literary curiosities about Easter Island, such as a travel book by John Dos Passos, the American novelist.

As for Brown's *Riddle of the Pacific*, it doesn't use today's terminology, but it seems to prefigure the storyline that most Easter Islandists agree on today: namely that local oral tradition is correct—that the arrival of outsiders on the island led to first a standoff between the newcomers, called the Long Ears, who built the moai in their own heavy-lobed image and were eventually defeated in a war that stopped moai construction dead and toppled the pieces already in place. For those dour stone heads so familiar to us today from films and still photos (and, in my own private crackpot theory, so important in modern art, as they represent the intersection of Amedeo Modigliani and Pablo Picasso) were all in fact re-erected in the twentieth century.

In the post-Brown era both radiocarbon dating and linguistic study show that the earliest human habitation dates from between 400 and 700 CE. The people, who wore tapa cloth and were tattooed, numbered from seven thousand to perhaps as many as twenty thousand. What they found on arriving was a dense subtropical environment that included a large palm that was kin to today's Chilean palm, which can reach a height of more than eighty metres and a girth of two. Vines supplied the material for rope. From these two came canoes large enough to allow for exploration. Easter Island is not surrounded by reefs. This exposure, and the cold water, make fishing difficult; it also causes the steep cliffs to erode, a problem that doubtless contributed to the ecological disaster. Statue construction reached its height at the start of the thirteenth century, eight hundred years after settlement, and probably ceased by the turn of the sixteenth. In other words, it was fading away, not rising, by the time Europeans colonized South America.

What happened? Studies of pollen and other research show that within four centuries of arrival the Polynesians were well into the irreversible process of denuding the island of its trees, probably for fuel, for houses, for ocean-going canoes, and for all the equipment needed to lever and roll the giant statues from the quarries where they were carved to the cliffs where they were erected, unquestionably for religious purposes. Engineers have shown how twenty people could carve such a statue in one year and could have manhandled the thing into position using slips and wooden derricks. This was an instance of titanism in religious art, such as one sees in the immense Buddha images of the kind I would encounter so often in Burma.

Trips across the sea resulted in the importation of chickens, which were consumed faster than they could reproduce. Rats hitched rides to the island as well, and these fed on the seeds of the coconut tree, hastening its disappearance. Shellfish and dolphins were overharvested, and whole species of birds wiped out. The inhabitants were now island-bound. They turned to cannibalism. Tradition and oral history tell of various devastating wars, especially that during which the Short Ears wiped out the Long, probably in the seventeenth century.

When Roggeveen visited the island in 1722, many of the statues were still standing. The next Europeans were the Spanish, in 1770, who called the place San Carlos, saw the stone houses, but noted that some of the people on the barren, windy place of waving grass and widely separated trees were living in caves. In 1774 Captain James Cook arrived with a Tahitian who was able to communicate with the people in his native tongue. Cook thought the moai belonged to a former civilization now extinct, and in a sense, of course, he was right. By this time, the monoliths were toppled, the people ill fed and poor. A French expedition in 1784 found them somewhat better off. A Russian counted twenty moai standing, so it seems their destruction wasn't an all-at-once affair, but a practice that resumed from time to time. Conditions waxed and waned, but the general trend was downward. Missionaries came and then, in 1862, the Peruvian blackbirders seeking slave labour for plantations and mines on the continent. About a thousand of the total population of perhaps four thousand were captured; of these, a thousand or so died of disease, overwork, or Christianity.

In 1877 a French sheep baron took over the island. This resulted in a war between capitalists, who wished to ship the native inhabitants to Tahiti, and the missionaries who, to their credit, were opposed. Many died over the issue. Capital won out. Only about a hundred islanders remained. Some of them rose up, killing the head of the French company. Between 1888, when the Chileans annexed the island in the expansionist frenzy of the Pacific War, and 1952, two years after the death of the last big tree on the island, Easter was leased to a Chilean-Scots sheep-grazing concern, which was supplanted by an all-Scots one until the Chilean navy took over. By that time, of course, Heyerdahl had made Easter Island a household name.

Mass tourism began only in 1967 with the opening of Mataveri Airport, which the islanders occupied in 1990 to protest a proposed fare hike by LanChile, their economic lifeline. At various periods the military restricted the islanders' travel and suppressed use of the Rapa Nui tongue. Pinochet had a plan to lease the airport to the United States as an emergency landing spot for the space shuttle. But with the restoration of democracy in Chile, life has become better for the Rapanui as well, though there was outrage when UNESCO designated the island a World Heritage Site without consulting them. Now there's local self-government. Some people talk of independence, but softly, for they know the muscle of the Chilean armed forces.

Poor Bernadette had been having so many difficulties, I had been relieved when she told me she would be staying on the mainland while I went to hell by sea, as she said she wished me to do. At first I was pleased to be headed for Easter Island alone. Later I was more honest with myself and admitted I missed her.

Because there are only two beaches, both on the north side, and no berths, just jetties, few turistas come by water, only a few hardy yachtsmen seeking an ultimate test of their abilities. Our arrival in the lumbering old troop ship was therefore an event of relative importance. The water was Vick's-bottle blue and perfectly calm, and I went ashore in our tender. The first Rapanui I saw was a teenage girl with two large tattoos, one of Jesus, the other of a lizard. She was among the hordes selling cheap handicrafts and general junk at the head of the jetty. A small party of us, maybe ten or eleven in all, struck out immediately for the nearest site of importance, Ahu Tahai, a short hike north of the decentralized town. Here three ahu were restored by William Mulloy in 1968. Mulloy is a more respected figure on the island than Heyerdahl, though no one denies Heyerdahl credit as the father of Easter Island tourism. From there we piled into a minibus for a drive to Rano Raraku, most interesting of the volcanoes, as it was the primary source of the rock from which the moai were carved. All the way up the steep switchback path to the summit one sees carved moai never freed from their place of manufacture, or else broken or split ones. Many of these giants, carved in the horizontal position, were left with their volcanic umbilicals unsevered when production suddenly stopped. Clearly a disproportionate amount of the island's wealth, resources, and man-power were expended at this spot, exacerbating the society's decline. The caldera is a reed-choked lake that gravity-feeds a small communal cistern below.

Rapa Nui has only two important roads, a partial ring road, which serves as the main street of Hanga Roa, and a more recent road, much of it paved, bisecting the island south to north. At the northern terminus are the two beaches, one much larger than the other, with frothy surf striking crescents of whitish sand. Visitors must be careful to swim only at the one with a breakwater, as the other is a haunt of tiger sharks. The party I was with took this road to reach Ahu Tongariki, the most famous postcard view of Easter

Island, with fifteen enormous moai standing shoulder to shoulder with their backs to the sea. To get there we passed through a land of small farms, which are handed down from grandfather to grandson once the latter has learned the secrets of when to plant by moonlight, where to find the biggest lobsters (most Chilean lobsters come from Easter Island), and so on.

Well-fed cattle are numerous. They blocked the roads as though in some organized protest. There are also about fifteen hundred horses on the island, looking quite healthy, despite what some guidebooks state, and all of them branded with symbols about twenty-five centimetres high in order that they may graze communally. They do so untended, and one of the few crime problems on Easter Island is horse rustling by the very poor who use the stolen animals for food (in preference to the cattle apparently). Large-scale reforestation has benefitted the island enormously, though most of the trees never attain mature stature and lumber, like all other building supplies, like indeed everything else, is brought from the Chilean mainland on the monthly supply ship. The most impressive work of agriculture I saw was a large orange grove. Mostly the island is subsistence agriculture and market gardening. "Life is hard here," said Ian (pronounced Jan), a native-born Rapanui who returned home after twenty years in the north of England. He speaks English during the tourist season when three or four smallish cruise ships call offshore. His accent is pure Norwich, though he is slowly forgetting his vocabulary.

"Like me, people need different jobs to support their family. When there are no tourists to take around, I fish, I grow food, raise a few animals. Like I say, life is hard here, but there's not much…" Someone has to supply the word. "Yeah, stress. That's it."

He took us to Tongariki and told us the recent history of this most famous of Easter Island sights. The gargantuan moai there once numbered more than fifteen. But in 1960 an undersea earthquake midway between the island and the mainland resulted in a tsunami that toppled the original chorus line, scattering all of them and smashing a number. The site lay in ruin until recent years when Japan offered to re-erect the remaining moai in return for borrowing one of the figures for a yearlong exhibition. When the time came to reinstate the moai, the Japanese used heavy cranes brought from Osaka. Local residents observed the work closely and now have small portable cranes they use to put up old moai here and there. Such processes, if unchecked, could quickly turn Easter Island into a theme park, particularly now that both the new airport as well as television have greatly increased the pace of the island as of only three years ago. The fact that forty-two percent of the island is a Chilean national park, however, has prevented, so far, an invasion by Rupert Murdoch or Disney or others of their kind.

I returned to the ship by tender at the end of the day, leaving from a kind of lightly sheltered inlet with a small fishing jetty: the only such facility on Easter. I no sooner sat down than I saw Bernadette's red hair. She had just got in on the four-hour LanChile flight from Santiago, feeling better now at least temporarily. Inevitably, for such crime is an important form of entrepreneurship in Santiago, she had had her handbag snatched but had managed to cancel and replace her credit cards. Luckily she also had kept her travel documents in a safe at the Carrera.

We agreed that the next day she would make a general all-day tour of the island, as visiting the place without seeing the highlights would be a pity and a shame. For my part I hired a horse at the jetty the next morning and set out for town, first to change money and then to call at the post office. Hitching my horse to a stanchion outside the post office was my silent rebuke to the world of e-mail. After exploring the town thoroughly, I turned south and rode up the grassy slope of Rano Kau, the volcano at the extreme southern tip of the island. The approach was steep and littered with porous volcanic rocks, but on the more level, pasture-like stretches I managed to provoke the horse, which had a Polynesian name that didn't register with me, to a cross between a canter and a stumble. We spent a truly carefree afternoon together, lunching on the cliffs overlooking the battering surf a couple of hundred metres below. Visibility was (I can only guess roughly) about sixty nautical miles, but one could go three thousand miles before encountering another piece of land. Some frigate birds whirled overhead.

I rode for an hour, then walked the horse for a quarter hour, repeating the process for the rest of the day. We rode through some seasonal rainstorms of great intensity and short duration. After the first one, I tied my hooded wind-cheater to the conchos on the saddle. There was no one around, and I sang folksongs at the top of my lungs, something I could never do in a city or a town. The horse seemed to wiggle his ears in what I chose to take as appreciation.

Horse and man were both due back at the jetty at 1700 when the former had to be returned to the stable and the latter had to catch the first tender to the ship, which had moved over to the other side of the island in order to rendezvous with a tanker and take on fuel. I was there on time and so were the others, but not the ship. We took shelter from the sun in the shade of an ahu on which we had seen islanders erecting a small moai with a truck-mounted crane earlier in the day. We waited for four hours. A serious storm seemed to be percolating. Lightning was crackling with increasing frequency not far offshore, where two squall systems were clearly visible. The sky began to darken prematurely.

By now a large crowd of us had assembled, but Bernadette was nowhere in sight. Some aloof types—we called them the Long Ears—stayed by themselves on a distant eminence, looking for the ship, while the rest of us, the majority, stayed close to the jetty, eyeing an open-sided metal building that housed a converted US Navy landing craft, thinking we could use the structure for shelter when the storm let loose. Our Greek captain, as it happened, had been delayed on the other side, arguing about the price of bunker-C. The ship didn't turn up until the last daylight began to fade. The five zodiacs weren't loaded until about 2100 or 2130, by which time it was dark and the water was acting up.

Zodiacs are considered unsafe at night, as they have no lights whatsoever, not even running lights, and they tend to fill with water in swells of a metre or more. Still the ship was about two nautical miles or so offshore. The rules were bent. Later I thought I could reconstruct what went on in the captain's mind. *Do I leave these people ashore for the night, buying up every spare bedroom on the island at a cost of many thousands? Or do I risk getting them aboard, knowing what I know from the radio and the weather fax?* What he knew that we didn't was that what had begun as a routine tropical squall was fast on its way to being confirmed as the worst storm to hit Easter Island in more than a generation.

I didn't know where Bernadette was, but I was in the second zodiac, sitting one and a half nautical miles out, waiting for our turn to approach the landing stage at the bottom of the gangway. Zodiac One was making the approach now while Three through Five bobbed round us along with the two eleven-metre tenders, which had wheelhouse construction and side curtains to lower. Soon the sea picked up to nearly two metres. With no cover we were absolutely soaked as the rain beat down on us and the waves crashed over the pontoons where we sat, nine of us including the sailor working the outboard. Every few seconds, on the crest, we could see the ship sitting there, wearing every light the electricians could string together. A few seconds later, on the downroll, we were plunged back between the waves, disoriented, neither ship nor island in sight. We hung on by means of a small-diameter line strung through grommets along the tops of the pontoons, thinking the same thought: we weren't going to make it.

The waves were thundering in, the water now just about over the tops of our shoes, but we couldn't shift our feet out of the way lest we destabilize the zodiac. I was thinking quickly but not clearly. Spying a five-gallon red plastic jerry can of gas, I wondered how long it would take me to cut it in half with the Swiss army knife in my pocket and make two bailers. But, of course, the problem wasn't that we would be swamped and sink. We couldn't sink in an inflatable unless we suffered punctures. The danger, rather, was that a wave would flip us over and capsize us, so that we'd land like a piece of toast falling to the floor jam-side down—a prospect that was becoming more and more likely as the waves grew higher, to the point where, for a few dreadful seconds each time, we were nearly at right angles to the horizon, alternately facing shipward or landward. Across from me a husband and wife embraced in what looked like a Hollywood farewell. Next to me a woman in her seventies held on to her cane ever more tightly; over the roar of the weather I could hear snatches of the prayers she muttered. The zodiacs were beginning to seem a poor idea. Every once in a while we'd catch a glimpse of one of the tenders. Although much sturdier, they weren't doing any better. The violence with which they were being lightly tossed about just left me knowing how much worse we must have seemed to them.

The first zodiac somehow got near enough to the ship to make a try for the gangway but was turned away. The captain was going to swing round on the chain to give the landing stage at the bottom better cover. We circled and circled and circled in the dark. A half hour. An hour. An hour and half. The full force of the storm was on us now. The zodiac skipper, an Argentine, tried to keep spirits up by singing nostalgic songs about Buenos Aires, of which he had an endless repertoire.

Finally Zodiac One made its first approach to the gangway, taking advantage of a very narrow window. Only three passengers managed to scramble aboard the ship before the flimsy aluminum platform broke. We could hear the confusion expressed in squelchy speech on the walkie-talkie pinned to our operator's slicker. Two sailors wearing no flotation devices whatsoever were attempting to fix the problem with a hand drill and bolts while hanging on with one hand.

"Greeks!" our tiller man finally said in exasperation. "They know nothing of the sea. *Nothing!*" I felt it wasn't the right time for me to mention Homer.

We all made attempts in turn, followed by the tenders, but to no avail. Now the question seemed to be not whether we would get aboard the mother ship but how many of us would end up in the water. Sailors had strung a bright orange lifeline more than half the length of the hull within a half metre of the waterline on the port-side. They also trained all their searchlights on our patch of the sea, but they weren't agile enough to stay focused on the targets. All of us in the zodiacs had life vests on, though not elaborate ones. Each did have a light and whistle. The people in the tenders had no personal flotation devices at all. It seemed only a question of time until the waves crashing over us loosened people's grips and sent us tumbling overboard. I was the youngest person in my raft, I believe, but I'm not a strong swimmer. I began to calculate how I might reach the orange lifeline if I didn't lose all sense of direction and begin to choke uncontrollably. A fellow passenger was now throwing up quite severely. I tried to puzzle out the problem of hypothermia. The water had been warm during the day, but the rain was cold and most of us were in T-shirts and shorts or might as well have been. I thought I might be able to wallow to the line if we happened to be in the right place in our elliptical circuit when the worst happened—say, no more than a few metres from the ship. I had no idea how I could help the prayerful septuagenarian with the walking stick.

Two local fishing boats about four metres long bravely came out to join us in the storm and presumably to pluck people out of the water if necessary. This showed great courage and charity on the part of the fishers. Then a small patrol boat appeared. Being thirty-five hundred kilometres offshore, Easter Island is obviously not claimed by Chile on the basis of propinquity, and a token naval presence is thought necessary to reinforce the country's claim to sovereignty. The patrol boat, a fibreglass affair, first stopped at the jetty to pick up twenty of our fellow passengers there. Having bow and stern thrusters, it could get close to our eerily lit ship; being higher than the gangway, it could, if the timing was exact, sort of hurl people one at a time down onto the platform from above. Over the next hour the Chilean sailors took aboard zodiac passengers but had to give up offloading us after the first three or four clambered aboard: conditions were worsening. So as many of us as could cram into the patrol boat did so and were returned to shore. Even this crossing was petty rough. The couple opposite me kissed again, but whether in deliverance or as a further gesture of farewell I couldn't tell. Once we were back on the jetty, the navy went out again and again until all the zodiacs and the tenders were empty and maybe a hundred and twenty-five of us joined the equally drenched people who had never left shore.

Locals drove us to the largest hotel in town, where I found Bernadette, soaked and bedraggled but otherwise fine, in the lobby, looking pissed off. She hadn't been able to see what was happening because of the storm, and when I told her about having to be rescued by the Chilean navy, she called me a liar. The crowd was far more than the little hotel could handle. There was nothing to drink and only a handful of blankets. People already had begun dossing down for the night on the floor of the lobby and the restaurant, even in the space beneath the billiard table. An American woman, who had stayed ashore the previous night at a bed-and-breakfast, said she could probably find us accommodation there. Nine couples, including Bernadette and me, set off, with Bernadette, the only one fluent in Spanish, the most valuable member of our party and, I say to her credit, the most unflappable. So eventually we were able to pull off our wet clothes, wrap ourselves in blankets, and get into dry beds. I woke frequently during the night because Bernadette was grinding her teeth from tension now that the crisis seemed to be over. I had just nodded off, irretrievably, I thought, when a rooster announced the imminence of dawn. We got back into our clothes, which were just as wet as when we left them, and walked down the hall to where fresh pineapple and instant coffee were laid out for us.

Bernadette and I both had bronchitis, but she refused to admit it, denying the fact between horrible-sounding coughs that punctuated every couple of words. Another of our group, who had Parkinson's disease and had left her medication aboard, looked as though she were in some sort of preshock. We settled our bill as best we could, using a colourful assortment of currencies, and made our way back to the inlet. Ambulances were standing by, but miraculously no one had drowned or even been injured: everyone made it back to the ship. Later on in the voyage, however, long after Bernadette and I disembarked at Papeete, there were three casualties. An elderly woman with a handicap was simply washed overboard without a trace during a storm in the Mediterranean. I couldn't help but wonder whether this was the woman with the cane with whom I'd shared a zodiac. Two people, I was later told, committed suicide without saying why.

Getting the purser to reimburse us for the out-of-pocket expenses of the bed-and-breakfast was an act of oral surgery requiring several days to complete. By that time the air was hot, the Pacific at its bluest and calmest, and we were near Pitcairn Island—twelve or thirteen thousand nautical miles, and sixty-two days, from where we started, close enough to my destination that I began to take my anti-malarials as prescribed.

Until the handover of Hong Kong in 1997 there were seven million residents of British colonies in the Pacific. Now there are only forty-four. They live on Pitcairn Island and most are descendants of the mutineers who took over the British ship *Bounty* from Captain William Bligh in 1789. Their little community has long had its ups and downs. But Pitcairners have had one constant in their collective lives for the past two centuries: isolation. That's what brought Fletcher Christian and his small band of fellow fugitives, and their Polynesian women, in the first instance: they were seeking an unpopulated place to hide.

They made a brilliant choice. Pitcairn is a little volcanic dot of only a few square kilometres. The nearest big inhabited places are thousands of klicks away. Few ships call at Pitcairn, as there is no moorage and the surf is so dangerous that only one in four attempts to get over the reef in small boats is successful. Still, trading with passing vessels has long been the lifeblood of the Pitcairn economy, along with philately and self-sufficient vegetable gardening. Now this may be changing.

Tom Christian, Fletcher's great-great-great grandson, is the island's elder statesman. He has been awarded an M.B.E. by the queen. Also, like most old-time sailors, he carries a sheath knife on his belt, right in the small of his back, so it's equally accessible with either hand. He is negotiating with the Foreign and Commonwealth Office in London for the British government to build the island's first airstrip. Such a facility would connect Pitcairn by air with the Outside—specifically with one of the farthest-flung islands of French Polynesia. Christian and his supporters on the island say the move is inescapable if Pitcairn society is to continue to exist at all, since its population has dropped to a mere sixteen households and it cannot lure back its younger generation once they've seen the bright lights of New Zealand. Others predict that if the field is built Pitcairn, which can boast of no hotels, restaurants, or tourism, will have a scuba-based economy within a couple of years, and a traditional way of life will be lost. Given these circumstances, I was eager to see Pitcairn for myself before it changed irrevocably.

The Pitcairn story needs little recapitulation, only a bit of correction. The Canadian-built replica of the *Bounty* used in the two most recent Hollywood films about the incident is far bigger than the original, which was never HMS *Bounty*, as it was scarcely big enough to be called a ship. Officially it was HMAV (His Majesty's Armed Vessel) or HMT (His Majesty's Transport); it had earlier been used to haul coal in Scotland. Bligh was captain of the ship but only a lieutenant by rank, so his first mate, Christian, an old family friend ten years his junior, was made an acting lieutenant for the purpose of the voyage. The destination was Tahiti, where the crew were to gather breadfruit trees for transplanting in the West Indies as a cheap food for slaves.

The mutiny took place not because of brutality on Bligh's part. He was a less extreme disciplinarian than Captain James Cook, his former commander. It took place rather because Bligh was too lax in allowing the crew to form relationships with Tahitian women. His men were thus reluctant to leave once the botanical errand was completed. In what appears to have been a spontaneous rather than a well-planned operation, Bligh and others were set adrift in a danger-ously overcrowded seven-metre open boat (which Bligh sailed almost four thousand nautical miles to Timor). Sixteen of those remaining on the *Bounty* elected to take their chances in Tahiti; three were eventually hunted down and hanged. Fletcher Christian, who was twenty-seven, sailed away, carrying nine seamen, twelve Tahitian women, six Tahitian men, and one baby girl.

Christian knew of the existence of Pitcairn, just below the Tropic of Capricorn, because it had been mentioned by Philip Carteret of the *Swallow* expedition. But the Admiralty chart misplaced it by two hundred nautical miles. Once he located it, Christian avoided detection by burning the ship at what's still called Bounty Bay (actually an inlet at best). The anniversary of the scuttling, 23 January, is Bounty Day on Pitcairn, the island's most important secular holiday. In 1808 an American whaling captain called at Pitcairn and found only one of the original mutineers alive. This was Alexander Smith, who had changed his name to John Adams and become the island patriarch, using the *Bounty*'s Bible and *The Book of Common Prayer* to teach the children to read and write. In 1884 the islanders were converted by Seventh Day Adventists from the United States.

Today the Adams role is filled by Tom Christian. I found him, at sixty-five, a well-educated man with Polynesian features but some of his famous ancestor's physique and colouring, for though no like-ness of Fletcher Christian was made from life (he was murdered about 1793), Bligh once described him in a letter as being "slim and dark-complected with sharp features." Nothing like Errol Flynn, Clark Gable, Marlon Brando, or Mel Gibson, the quartet who have played him in movies.

Pitcairn's population peaked in 1936 at two hundred and thirty-six (this after several British initiatives in the nineteenth century to relocate the Pitcairners on Tahiti or on Norfolk Island, midway between New Zealand and Australia). Today the Pitcairners are administered from Whitehall via the British high commissioner in Wellington, who doubles as governor of Pitcairn, a place he is expected to visit at least once during his three-year term, possibly wearing his ceremonial sword and plumed hat on special occasions. A supply ship from New Zealand reaches Pitcairn every few months, and its cargo must be taken ashore by the Pitcairners in two aluminum launches, also acquired from New Zealand.

Our own ship was hove-to half a mile offshore, close enough to see the landing place and the Hill of Difficulties behind it. This sounds like a name from *Pilgrim's Progress*—through the Slough of Despond, up the Hill of Difficulties, turn left at the video shop. In fact, it is the road that leads to the settlement, Adamstown, where the co-op store, town hall, and church are located. There is also a jail, but it has never been used. "Most of my work is settling the occasional domestic dispute," the resident female constable told me. According to a British travel writer, Dea Birkett, in her 1997 book *Serpent in Paradise*, a work that still rankles with Pitcairn people, the main occupation is malicious gossip.

Approaching the island, we communicated with Tom Christian by radio. He trained in marine electronics in New Zealand and is in charge of the island's communications. He advised that we could find calmer water on the southern side of the island. So we steamed round landmarks with such names as Where Freddie Fall and the

Pool of Uaru to an indentation in the coastline called the Rope. There we anchored and awaited the islanders to come to us in one of the motor launches. Almost everybody came, including the children, leaving only three or four people on land. They set up tables to sell their handicrafts and wares. They also bartered with the ship itself, swapping great heaps of fresh fruit and vegetables for scores of old pillows and ten surplus mattresses.

"When I was going to school," Christian said, "we were forbidden to speak the local language." It's called Pitkern, and it combines Polynesian words with archaic English words such as *gwen* ("gone") and *yonder* (used without affectation), all with simplified constructions. Speaking among themselves, Pitcairners might ask, "About you going?" or "What why you?" *Tedside* is a contraction for "the other side" and *yolly* is the local equivalent of "y'all."

"I went away to study," Christian continued, "but have been back on Pitcairn since 1955. I guess I've held most of the official jobs, including that of magistrate" (now called mayor). At one time Pitcairn had sixteen registered amateur radio operators, the highest per capita concentration in the world. Christian is still a ham operator: his call sign is VP6TC; his wife Betty's is VP6YL. He speaks to many passing ships and to Pitcairnophiles round the world, or "round the whorl," as he pronounces it. The island has a Web site too. So the world is closing in, but Pitcairn is embracing it.

"Betty and I have four girls," Christian said. "Only one went to university. She's now a pharmacist in Sydney. Another is a hairdresser in Auckland. In 1953 my fifteen-year-old sister died of a burst appendix when we couldn't get help in time. We watch videos, but there's no TV reception. I've tried experimenting with it but haven't been able to pick up anything." As it is, the major recreations are films and occasional cricket matches. The matches last two days.

In all there are a hundred and sixty thousand residents in Britain's few remaining colonies. The others are in the Atlantic or the Caribbean: Anguilla, Bermuda, the British Virgin Islands, the

Cayman Islands, the Falklands, Gibraltar, Montserrat, St. Helena, Ascension, Tristan da Cunha, and the Turks and Caicos. Until the present Labour government these were called dependent territories and some of the residents (generally speaking, the white ones) had first-class British citizenship while others held only second-class. Now these scattered remnants are called overseas territories and their citizens are full British subjects, with all the rights and privileges appertaining thereto. The change has been necessary to bring British policy in line with that of other European Union countries, notably France, the Netherlands, and Denmark.

Right now Pitcairn Island has a healthy surplus in its bank account, but the price of isolation is spiralling and the British government is of little help, critics charge. Pitcairn is one of four bits of land lying in the Tuamotu Archipelago, surrounded by French Polynesia. The largest of them is Henderson Island, a hundred and ten nautical miles to the east—low, flat, and without fresh water. In the late 1980s an American coal-mine-owning millionaire from Frog Level, Virginia, hit on Henderson while cruising the world in his yacht. He was said to be seeking a place to found a colony based on anti-Semitism, hatred of African-Americans, and loathing of psychiatrists. He asked the British government to sell the island to him but was rebuffed. Then he offered to lease it for ninety-nine years for £5 million, promising to build a modern airport and, what's more, to give Pitcairners a large motor vessel of their own. The government of the time almost went through with the deal, stopping only because of vigorous protests by the World Wildlife Federation, which pointed out that Henderson is home to unique species of birds, including a flightless rail and a fruit-eating pigeon. Tom Christian and others, however, blame a mealy-mouthed Foreign and Commonwealth Office for killing the plan.

"We need an airstrip to keep the island alive," he explained simply the day we were there. "We all have generators and freezers. The price of a kilowatt hour of electricity has gone up from twenty cents to fifty cents" in New Zealand currency. "Freight costs have increased almost as much. It now costs $6,000 to get a ship to land with supplies, quite apart from the cost of the freight itself. At the present rate the revenue will run out by the year 2006." So may the most valuable resource: children. "Once someone has been away to learn a trade, they find there's no future on the island," he said.

Christian told us he hoped that before 2001 was out a team of British military engineers would have used up a precious patch of Pitcairn's arable land to construct a short gravel airstrip big enough to connect Pitcairn to the nearest and so far uninhabited island of French Polynesia, four hundred and eighty kilometres away in the Gambiers. "The airstrip is not just a good thing," he said. "It's something we consider essential, for without it Pitcairn will be even harder to keep going. We still like the life. We have a lot of freedom. But there's a question of whether we can continue. You people think we who live on a small tropical island sit under the palm trees all day. It isn't like that."

Their handicraft sales and bartering complete at the end of a long day, the Pitcairners, romantic descendants of people who defied the mightiest nation of the day and got away with it, loaded their longboat. As the lines were cast off and they pulled away, they all joined in singing the traditional song of farewell: "Now one last song we'll sing/Goodbye, Goodbye/Time moves on rapid wings/Goodbye, Goodbye, Goodbye." The lyrics, many fear, had taken on a special poignancy of late. And there the matter would have rested in my memory if, long after returning to Vancouver, I hadn't read in the newspapers about the child molestation scandal that rocked Pitcairn to its core.

THREE PAGODAS PASS

*O*ur health, physical and psychological, Bernadette's and mine, improved the moment we left the ship as planned at Papeete in Tahiti, where it put in to take on six hundred tonnes of fuel. Papeete's local newspaper, which runs photographs of deformed vegetables and people departing for holidays abroad, covered the arrival of the vessel, which it called a *"véritable monument historique."* Quite. Papeete, which because of its colonial soul might be called the French equivalent of Port Stanley, looked pretty good after two months at sea. Such was the way it had always looked in those circumstances. But its charms, including the entire island of Mooréa, began to evaporate after five days—again as per custom.

The town seemed to have fallen on hard times since I was there a few years earlier. The reason was everywhere to be seen. Prices, already high, had risen alarmingly. Local telephone calls, for example, were sometimes ten American dollars. Papeete was simply pricing itself out of business and becoming a sort of holding tank for holiday-makers bound for Mooréa, Bora Bora, and elsewhere. Fewer and fewer of the big liners such as the *QE2* were calling there, and many shop fronts along the Boulevard Pomare sat vacant. The place would be desolate without the huge administrative and military payrolls. Bernadette and I sat on the penultimate floor of my favourite harbour-side dump of a hotel taking turns looking through binoculars at the comings and goings of French warships.

We filled out French immigration cards on arrival and were supposed to check off the reason for our visit: holiday, business, "Honey Moon." I put a mark beside *autre*. I thought I dealt pretty well with Bernadette's flares of temper, just as I handled their meteorological equivalents, the daily tropical showers, during which it rained like hell without warning but for only ten minutes each day. One night, however, she got into a real stew, accusing me of neglecting her and also of showing more affection to a dog the previous day than I had to her (the dog *was* a pretty amiable fellow, but I'd merely spoken to him for a few moments without even petting). The argument promised to go on all night unless there was some action on my part. So at about 2200 hours I took one pillow and the counterpane and made my bed on the floor near the door. This caused her to charge out onto the balcony and chain-smoke for an hour with special resentment. Eventually, though, she came in and climbed into bed. All was well until the fire alarm went off at 2300. I dressed and took the filthy stairwell to the lobby to investigate, reminding Bernadette not to use the lift if this turned out to be a real fire. Once the Chinese manager told me the alarm was false, I returned to my pillow to sleep. An hour later the alarm sounded again, and the lobby filled with people such as myself. The manager explained that drunken soldiers were moving from floor to floor, turning in bogus alarms. "Everything is okay," he said. "Nothing to worry." I urged him to turn off the system with his key, which he did.

The hotel was so much on its uppers that, except for the hooting of the ferries directly across the esplanade, our room was normally silent, because the rooftop bar above us had gone out of business. Since Quinn's Tahitian Hut, another landmark of intrigue, had closed in 1973, this had been the most notorious drinking spot in the South Pacific. The hotel's casino was dark as well, leaving Papeete with only a dozen or so. So it was with a sense of decay all round me that on our last evening in town I was forced next door to have a nightcap. To judge from the others' youth, haircuts, and general appearance, I was the sole patron not in the French military. Certainly I was the only one not trying to impress at least one and sometimes two Polynesian transgendered prostitutes lounging beneath the image of Céline Dion that filled the wall-size video screen. A few hours later Bernadette and I parted and departed, she for Vancouver via Los Angeles, I to Thailand and Burma by the typically circuitous route of Auckland and Sydney.

To make a long journey short, Burma was the point of my trip and I couldn't have chosen a worse time for it. In terms of weather, conditions were ideal along the always interesting and occasionally fluid Thai-Burmese border. Politically, however, I had come at a poor moment. Like the British before them, the junta, growing even more repressive as it becomes still richer from opium and methamphetamines, has the tightest control only of the wide valley of the Irrawaddy, from far above Mandalay in the north to Rangoon in the south. On either side of this wide riverine right-of-way, ownership is more ambiguous. The various hill peoples—the Chin, the Karen, the Kachin, the Shan—continue to hold sway over their own lands to one degree or another and to practise their own customs, which include resistance to the central authorities. This is as much as one can generally say about them, for they really are distinct individual cultures, some of Indian heritage, others of Tibeto-Burman origin. In the 1990s the Kachin Independence Army finally folded, but some armed resistance continues elsewhere in the country.

The paragraph above is only the broadest possible statement of where matters stood when I began planning my trip, at which time two significant events took place. First, signs of insurgent activity began springing up in the supposedly secure central river valley, scaring the hell out of the junta. The generals long ago had beaten back the ethnic insurgents into remote mountain areas of ever-decreasing size, a campaign made easier by the racism rampant among the ethnic Burmans towards the so-called hill tribes. Now here were some of their own kind, albeit students, pro-democracy crackpots poisoned by western values, committing a few scattered acts that couldn't be dismissed as mere political theatre. Their deeds sent the political equivalent of malarial tremors through the general staff in Rangoon. Second, in October, just as I was making my travel plans, twenty-five members of a Burmese student group, its militant side previously unknown to the junta, occupied the Burmese embassy in Bangkok to highlight the nonexistence of democracy back home. The takeover of this bleak and prisonlike building at 132 Th Sathon Neva was brought to a peaceful conclusion by the Thai authorities. But the incident had the effect of moving both countries to shut down the few remaining legal crossing points along their common border. In order to step over the line of demarcation I would require on-the-spot information, for whatever appeared in the press was already out-of-date no doubt.

Such was the situation on the day I was preparing to fly from Sydney to Bangkok when an event took place of which I was unaware at the time. The group that had usurped the embassy in Bangkok, a band named the Vigorous Burmese Student Warriors, executed a joint mission with another body, a Karen splinter faction calling itself God's Army and led by twin twelve-year-old boys who were said to possess mystical powers and who smoked the enormous homemade cheroots the Burmese consume so avidly. This unlikely combined force of only ten captured the local hospital in Ratchaburi, the sleepy capital of the province of the same name in western Thailand, a short distance from the easternmost refugee camps that are home to a hundred thousand Karen and others who have fled Burma and its harshness for the democratic and prosperous monarchical state of Thailand. Patients and staff were held hostage. This was too much for the Thais, who after offering the Burmese a chance to surrender, retook the building by force, apparently using methods taught them by the United States. The charismatic young twins somehow escaped, vanishing in a way that reinforced their reputation for supernatural gifts. The other insurgents were taken prisoner and then, in what became a national scandal once Thailand's press, the freest in Southeast Asia, got hold of the story, were executed on the spot, one by one, with bullets to the head.

This extrajudicial killing was what one would expect in Burma, not Thailand, and was widely interpreted as a change in policy on the part of the Thais, who until then had permitted the large refugee community to exist along its side of the border as a useful buffer against the unpredictable Burmese military (who despite this sometimes made punitive incursions against the camps). To many Thais, both within the government and without, the refugees now seemed to be attracting more trouble than they were worth. By the time I arrived, a backlash against them was all too obvious in the Thai media, and the border was closed tight. How was I going to get a firsthand albeit furtive look at conditions inside Burma?

On arrival I didn't linger in Bangkok but straightaway headed upcountry, a term Bangkokese use for any part of Thailand that isn't theirs, regardless of the direction shown on the compass. My first destination was the Three Pagodas Pass, the southernmost of only a very few breaks in the mountain range separating Thailand from Burma, or linking them, depending on your point of view. As a route for smugglers, the pass was already ancient in the days of the spice trade. Its military importance is similarly timeless almost beyond measure. Century after century the Chinese and their various traditional enemies, such as the Vietnamese and the Burmans, used it to send invading armies back and forth. Well into the age of modernity, the king of Siam employed it to dispatch armoured war elephants into Burma. The closest match I could manage with what must have been the world's heaviest, slowest, and most fearsome cavalry was one of the buses of the Baw Khaw Saw, the government coach line that helps hold Thailand together. The blue-and-red ones are first class, the blue-and-orange second class, and the orange-and-white third class. At the Southern Terminal I boarded a third-class one, meaning that, although it had air-conditioning, it was a slow, flatulent vehicle that stopped along the way whenever anyone appeared by the side of the highway to flag it down, as happened frequently. These latecomers included a man wearing a jungle-pattern camo shirt above the waist and a loud blue *longyi* below, and a toothless woman smoking a cheroot the size of a medium carrot. A third passenger wore a leather shoulder rig for his money and papers, as indeed I did too. The difference was that I wore mine under my shirt so as not to draw attention whereas his was on the outside. Perhaps he was proud of its fine tooling (the workmanship was of the highest standard). Or perhaps he was daring people to mess with him, announcing that any thief would have to kill him in the course of a robbery.

Much had improved in Bangkok since I was there last, and much had deteriorated. There were far fewer tuk-tuks and even more auto-mobiles. More people were literally jumping aboard the fast taxis that ran up and down the few remaining klongs, where for twenty baht, it seemed to me, not knowing where I was going, a person could ride forever. There was greater prosperity but more poverty, with the homeless sleeping on the pavement within sight of the trendy little waterside homes. In general there was simply more of everything, especially people and traffic and pollution. Bangkok was only partway through its ten-year skytrain-building project. There's nothing like building an elevated railway to make rush hour even more complicated, especially in a city where elephants parade at night so that citizens may buy food for them and thus increase the merit balances in their karma accounts. Which is to say that it took us what seemed an eternity before we had crossed the city to the westbound highway leading to the kind of semi-rural no-man's-land of pottery shops and isolated temples. In time we hit the bedroom community of Nakhom Pathorn, which lies about midway between the low plain and the place where the mountains suddenly appear on the horizon like pages in a pop-up book.

Between there and the significantly charmless city of Kanchanaburi, round which there had been fighting not that long ago, was strange territory in this, the dry season. Brittle grass punctured brown dry soil full of mosquitoes, scorpions, and yellow-headed termite-like creatures. What grew best was sugarcane. "The people get three harvests from one planting," someone told me. "Then they must burn the fields and start over." Swidden agriculture is still common in Thailand, especially at higher elevations than this. Sometimes we would pass little fires by the highway or see big balloons of wood smoke on distant hills, and I never knew whether these were deliberate or simply the seasonal brush fires caused by carelessness. I asked my intermittent interlocutor, apparently the only other English speaker on the bus. "Oh, the second is true, I believe," he said. As all across East Asia, you see industry being practised on all scales. Near one of the large sugar refineries, elderly women beat bunches of cane on the paved highway, as though trying to punish the concrete for some misdeed. This was how they make brooms, which they sell in the town markets for a few baht.

Naturally enough no one behind the counter at the bus station had been able to tell me how long it would take to get to the pass. Given a decently paved two-lane highway most of the way, I estimated seven hours. Unfortunately, the ticket sellers also neglected to tell me that the third-class bus only went as close as Kanchanaburi, a place attractive to tourists of a certain generation, as it is the point of departure for the Bridge on the River Kwai (actually Khwae) or rather the reconstruction of same, which is much smaller in reality than the Hollywood one remains in memory. From Kanchanaburi only two buses each day go northwesterly into the mountains. By the sheerest of stupid luck, I caught one of them after a wait of only an hour or so, spent wandering among the market stalls, where the main items of produce seemed to be corn, peanuts, potatoes, and lottery tickets, though there were stall holders specializing in everything from firewood to stuffed toys.

I lack the descriptive power to portray the mountains properly. They are not like mountains in Chinese painting. Neither are they like sharp volcanic ridges. But they have elements of both. They always seem to be present, looking down over your shoulder, but they take a long time to come into focus, sitting instead on the horizon like collage mountains torn from black paper and pasted onto a light blue background. Here are great knobs and knurls of grey porous rock, barren-looking that time of year but obviously covered in a jungly growth during the wet season, judging by the bamboo and vines that seem to crawl out to meet them across the empty country. As the bus rattled closer, I would see caves in the nearest mountain—and rank after rank of them queued up behind. I didn't have a topographical map, but the elevation seemed to be above a thousand metres at this point, rising to perhaps twice that as we rushed past two huge lakes, the reservoirs of hydro dams actually, where whole communities of fisher folk live in stilted huts far from shore. Here and there the road (it was rapidly ceasing to be a secondary highway) bore evidence of massive mud and rock slides from the previous wet season. At length we arrived at Sangkhlaburi where the bus stopped. I was given to understand that this was as far as foreigners were permitted, or perhaps as far as they dared. I wasn't confident I understood the subtleties.

Even in less tense times two certainties can be relied on. That the Thais and the Burmese don't care much for each other. That journalists and writers of all sorts are not permitted inside Burma except for the purpose of promoting a few hard-currency tourist spots, and even such permission as that is often revoked. Bertil Litner, the brilliant Burma correspondent of the *Far Eastern Economic Review*, a person who appears to have sources inside the government others would kill for (and possibly have), seems rarely if ever to set foot inside Burma officially, to judge by his writings. Which of course fools no one. But he is in a dangerous business in a place where writers are imprisoned as a matter of policy and often tortured. So it was that

I was travelling in my more familiar roles as a student of sacred architecture and buyer of uncut gemstones. Many of the world's emeralds and most of its rubies, including all the most desirable ones, come from Burma. I had taken the precaution of studying the subject and taking a little course with a gemological society, which resulted in a card with my name on it. The card—one could hardly call it a document—might be enough to fool someone not familiar with such matters but I was hoping that, along with the jeweller's loupe I carried and the terminology I could spout, I might be able to convince someone who speaks another language and, in any event, knows even less about gems than I do.

Because it had always been a kind of free-market no-man's-land, the Pass was the obvious place for me to test the current level of tolerance, though I wasn't sure how I was going to be greeted. In more normal times foreigners are permitted to cross into Burma for an hour's shopping on payment of five American dollars. Now, with the newspapers full of stories about the border being zippered up tight as the hunt for terrorists continued, I didn't know what I would be facing. For a lift to the Pass I traded my two brand-new shirts to the driver of an empty Japanese four-by-four, a Thai who I assumed was bound for Burma to buy a load of cheaply made teak or rosewood furniture. Since Thailand banned teak logging a decade ago, or drove it underground, this was said to be a lucrative trade for all concerned, including local police. The prohibition came at about the same time the Mon Liberation Front, which traditionally controlled the Pass and exacted tribute from anyone using it, fought a spirited war against the Karen National Union for the right to continue doing so. The results were that Payathonzu, the frontier town on the far side of the Pass, was destroyed, as the junta, taking advantage of the in-fighting, wrested control of the area for itself. But then Payathonzu was used to being destroyed in conflicts now and then.

The present situation was that the three pagodas—to westerners a misnomer, for actually they are rather only white chedis a couple of metres high, once covered in gold but now coated in stucco and said to contain relics of particularly revered monks—are on Thai territory, along with a tea shop and a few market stalls. Most of the vendors, who are Burmese, deal in the notorious furniture that is made before the wood has been properly dried and so is bound to crack and split. Others sell old military fatigues of uncertain origin but with Thai shoulder flashes tactfully sewn on, old and new helmets of both the Kevlar and straw varieties, a generous selection of knives and swords, and what I would have thought to be a nearly useless item: lightweight brass knuckles, in fact made of aluminum. All this was in addition to the wood carvings, fake Rolexes, glass gemstones, cigarette lighters, and general pieces of junk that are the trade goods of the modern world. At least no one at Three Pagodas Pass sold T-shirts printed with THREE PAGODAS PASS, for this is still thankfully more of a black market than a souvenir stand. In some places history still obtains.

The buildings that interested me were the Thai border police station on one side of the imaginary line, and the Burmese military checkpoint, complete with its red wooden barrier, currently lowered for the indefinite future. I asked the least unfriendly of the Thais if I could cross over into Burma. He said no, that wasn't permitted in the present atmosphere, it was too dangerous for foreigners. I kept rephrasing the question, politely and with modifications. His voice lowered but his tone sharpened. No hope, I thought he said, not with the general here doing his inspection. But there was no general, no other Thai military of any kind, no army vehicles in sight, much less any VIPs. So I stepped to the red barrier and asked permission to speak to a Burmese soldier a few metres away at the place I would normally have paid my $5 fee, as indicated on a sign in three languages. He was wearing camos and a black beret and carrying an M-16 in the carbine format that many profess to find useful for close-in work. He put his hand on the firearm. I was surprised that it looked so old, given how freshly and famously the Burmese had been rearmed. Actually, for a few seconds, before I moved away from the gate, I became transfixed by the weapon. During the Vietnam War, it was axiomatic that at the first opportunity some US soldiers would ditch the M-16s they had been issued in favour of the Russian-made AK-47, a simpler and more reliable weapon, more durable and less prone to jamming in humid conditions. Here we were more than a full generation later and the world was divided by brand loyalty as well as by every sort of racial, ethnic, religious, and political difference. Both the American M-16 and the Russian Kalashnikov designs were now being knocked off by any number of nations with no respect for intellectual property. Both weapons had undergone improvements as they became cheaper and more ubiquitous. For only US$5 million or so, not much as the cost of hardware is reckoned, a person can buy twenty thousand of either type, including spare parts and, with a little shrewd bargaining, virtually unlimited ammunition: enough to arm a considerable force indeed. Some always would choose the ripoff of the American technology while others inevitably would pick the AK-47 or one of its younger siblings, two of whose banana clips can be joined together with duct tape for twice its rival's load. Like PC and Mac users, or Coke and Pepsi drinkers, never the twain shall meet. One day there will be a war between people separated by nothing more than such preferences in the tools of war.

At length the Thais and the Burmese conferred and found a way, they thought, to put me off: a rare instance, it seems to me, of Thai-Burmese cooperation. The head Thai had appointed himself the spokesman for this unlikely ad hoc coalition, as his Burmese opposite number professed to have only one word of English: *foreigner*. There are numerous categories of visa and visa-like documents used in Burma. One is actually called a caravan trader's visa (don't ask). In Thailand too the paperwork is complex. Now I was told that to pay my fee to step over the line I would need to secure what is known as a frontier pass from the police back in the last town,

Sangkhlaburi, and return with it, complete with three passport photos, a photocopy of the first page of my passport, and a copy of the page showing my Thai visa stamp, in order to be permitted to leave Thai soil or to cross back over from Burma if I managed to get in.

I started to walk down the road I had come. After about a half hour, I flagged a Thai driving a truck full of lime-green melons the size of volleyballs and paid him three hundred baht to take me into town. There I got the proper form from the police and found a working photocopier and even someone to take Polaroid passport photos, as soon as we shooed the chickens out of her studio, which was located behind a garage yard full of rusty oil drums and worn-out tires. Then I hired a taxi for the long drive back, arriving to the evident surprise of the Thai authorities, who obviously felt they had seen the last of me. They took their time examining all the paperwork but finally permitted me to pass across the shadow thrown by the barrier and speak to the Burmese directly, officially.

I started at the beginning, pointing to the trilingual sign and asking to pay my $5 to the Burmese personnel inside the sentry station. Standing at the counter, I could see there were four of them, one in uniform, two mostly in mufti, and one who was half and half—below the level of the countertop he was in old sweatpants, above the line of sight in a crisply pressed uniform tunic. The one in full uniform was older than the others, who looked like kids to me. He was obviously the officer commanding this wretched little post, though he wore no insignia. He told me no, the border was closed. I tried every persuasive argument I could think of. He wouldn't budge. In fact, after a while he refused even to look up from a ledger in which he was writing while standing at the counter. Then he simply stopped answering my questions. I wandered off to think. What I came up with, squatting in the shade, was to wait him out until the shift changed and he was relieved by someone who might be more accommodating. I waited a couple of hours without the shift changing. I began to consider how I might sneak into Payathonzu, circling round behind it somehow, staying away from the road. After serious consideration, I decided this was impractical. There was a valid reason for the road's existence: the country on either side was impassable. And if I did manage to get to Payathonzu, I dare not show my face without being arrested for certain.

At this point, with the number of daylight hours becoming limited, I did the only wholly stupid thing I would do for the next month (for me, not a bad record, this—one foolish act every thirty days): I decided to practise the art of tea money. I returned to the Burmese military hut and presented myself again to the officer, who once more didn't glance up from his paperwork and showed no discernible expression, though I thought I knew the look of annoyance and hatred he was wearing inside. I again pleaded my innocence of every vice save respectful curiosity about his wonderful country, far-famed for its gentle ways and rugged beauty, and wondered whether I might be permitted to venture into Payathonzu under escort. Of course, I realized this would be an extracurricular chore for whoever escorted me, but I saw no reason why the person charged with such a duty should be penalized for taking on the extra task. In addition to a few baht and my US$5 bill, I had a carefully folded a US$50 note in the watch pocket of my jeans for emergencies. This was maybe three months' salary for a young solider, far too much money for the purpose at hand, bound to raise even more suspicions and set off alarms in ways that a ten or even a twenty might not. But it's what I had. I put the money on the countertop with all the casualness I could muster, unfolded it neatly, smoothed out the creases, and showed it to the Burmese, who looked at it but didn't touch it and, as before, betrayed no reaction. What must he have thought? I asked again, not knowing how much of what I said was getting through, whether an innocent traveller such as myself could hire an off-duty solider, perhaps during his dinner break, to accompany me that far, thus allaying any concern for my well-being. I feared I was only giving him more proof of his suspicions. Was I insulting him by displaying all this wealth like a callow westerner? Was I causing him to lose face somehow? I couldn't imagine *what* was going through his mind: I might have been asking if he had two twenty-fives in change. His left hand was as close to the greenback as his other was to his weapon.

Here is where my foolhardiness flowered. Since he didn't touch the note, I picked it up and tore it in half, straight down General Grant's nose, and gave him one half while I kept the other. Aside from the storm off Easter Island, this was the only point in my journey where I actually felt in physical danger. But after pausing for a few pregnant seconds, and still without changing expression or, it seemed to me now, assuming any expression at all, he took his half and stuck it between the pages of his ledger, then turned to confer with his subordinates. He understood completely. He assigned me one of his boy soldiers to take me where I wanted to go and leave me there. So, a bit like Charlie Chaplin at the end of his films, I walked out of view down the road to Payathonzu in what is officially Mon State, except I was accompanied by this teenager who, when he got tired of carrying his weapon, let the stock drag in the dust behind him.

At once I was struck by the poverty of the village. I had expected it to look newer as it had been rebuilt so recently. But, no, it appeared as though it had been rebuilt with the original materials and it seemed a hundred years old. Dirty children begged on the street under the teak sign boards on the fronts of the shops selling a narrow selection of goods despite the fact that this was a village rather than a mere crossroads. The emphasis was clearly on subsistence. Women with faces painted with white paste, a primitive sunscreen as well as an art form in Burma, breast-fed their infants or, in one case, dozed on the bare floor of a stall, taking a cue from the dogs that slept in whatever shade they could find. Still, there was much of interest to buy: military stuff, smuggled prescription drugs from Yunnan in China, smuggled knockoff electronics from Singapore via Bangkok, not to mention posters of Céline Dion. The most interesting goods were rubies and emeralds. As with the medicines, a person would have trouble both getting them out of Burma and into Thailand. Because of the gem trade, the Burmese are far more likely to search visitors on their way out of the country than on their way in.

Thai maps showing details of the Burmese side of the border indicate no other settlements beyond this one, but Burmese maps denote a couple of other villages farther along. Leaving my chaperon behind, I walked until the road became a track and threatened to become a mere gesture, at which point Burmese soldiers appeared to yell imprecations and motion at me with their beloved assault rifles. As I returned to Thai soil, I saw the only sign on the Burmese side in English. It read GOOD LUCK. I made a punctilious though low-keyed display of pausing at the soldiers' hut and giving the officer the other piece of the fifty. He accepted it without acknowledging its existence. My guess is he probably kicked back two dollars or so to the private. On the Kanchanaburi bus back to Bangkok the next night I saw narrow strips of fire raging in the mountains. From a distance the fire look like molten lava slithering down an erupting volcano.

A couple of days later, after recharging in Bangkok, I set out on another, longer trip to test conditions at some other point on the Burmese border. One idea was to go to Mae Hong Son in the northern province of the same name, where the morning mists make the hills appear to smoulder (memories of Tierra del Fuego). This is an area where tourists were often terrorized by dacoits in the 1980s but is now long pacified. As a result, the little city had become a muster point for trekkers grown weary of tripping over one another at Chiang Mai to the east, seeking out the hill tribes, especially the Karen, Muser, Lisu, Lahy, and Hmong, in order to get in touch with the primitive, or whatever phrase was current at the time. Instead I decided to head straight north through Chiang Mai to the slightly less tarted-up Chiang Rai, following the path already being abandoned by the eco- and ethno-tourists. My destination was the once-notorious

Golden Triangle region, specifically the town of Mae Sai, the most northerly place in Thailand. There, getting into Burma was a simple matter of crossing a short bridge on the principal street and hiking as far as Kengtung, only about a hundred klicks or so shy of the southernmost reaches of China.

I took my time, even though I was in a race not to get caught up in the travel chaos of Chinese New Year when the Year of the Rabbit would give way to the Year of the Dragon and hotels everywhere would be thronged, for although many of the Chinese resident in Mae Sai are Muslims, the majority are visitors or illegal aliens from Yunnan. I boarded the morning train from Hualamphong Station in Bangkok (air-conditioned second class, quite comfortable) and was in Chiang Mai not long after sunset. The track zigzags east and west, west and east, as it ascends the country, passing through many small cities as well as vast rural areas between. I saw more of a plant I had seen often on the Three Pagodas trip, a long bare stock, in extreme cases as high as a two-storey building, topped by a blossom that looked like a feather duster. One passenger in the carriage was carrying the *Asian Wall Street Journal* as well as Thai newspapers, and I made bold to ask him what the species was.

"Thai people call it communist plant," he said, "because when the wind blows it spreads to all parts."

I thanked him with the exaggerated politeness Thais both proffer and crave, and began reading a novel I had brought along. Much later, when we were in higher, wilder country, he spoke again, pointing out, as a matter of interest to the visitor, the rings of hard blue plastic wrapped round the wooden hydroelectric poles perhaps four metres off the ground. These, he explained, were to prevent snakes from crawling all the way up to the insulators and shorting out a circuit.

In Chiang Mai I spent the night at a cheap guest house with cigarette burns on the furniture, catching an early-morning bus to Chiang Rai, a place to which a number of prosperous Bangkokers are moving to escape noise and pollution, not noticing, apparently, any overcommercialization, at least not on the scale they're accustomed to. From there I travelled another sixty kilometres or so to Mae Sai, which isn't very commercialized, not in the touristy sense, but which certainly thrives on commerce, most of it conducted outdoors. I found a Chinese hotel built on an east-west axis and asked for a room on a top floor with a window facing north. The request was puzzling to the front desk. The manager had to be brought into the discussion, but he ruled in my favour, not quite understanding. I was given a key and a handbill outlining the hotel's amenities with needless hyperbole. "To fulfill [*sic*] your happiness," it read, "we offer you the choices of extensive menu of Thai and international dishes from experienced chefs, accompanied by sweet music and various entertainments designed to delight the ideal place." This meant that the hotel had a tea and noodle shop and permitted prostitutes to loiter in the lobby. "For those who prefer more tumultuous jollity," the writer continued, flipping madly through his or her thesaurus, "the pub disco gives the pleasure of the most sophisticated lighting in the North."

My insistence on a north-facing room paid off. From my window I could see the point, two blocks away, at which the town of Mae Sai, Thailand, melted into the town of Tachilek, Burma, famous market for illegal armaments and most everything else. In fact, all the landmarks—the shopping plazas, the new Catholic church painted to look as though it were made of red brick, the golden Shwedagon Pagoda, which the faithful reach by an arduous climb— were on the other side of the blue sign that read WELCOME TO THE UNION OF MYANMAR—ANY WEAPONS MUST NOT BE CARRIED. The wording put me in mind of the great Fats Waller: "Please check your firearms at the door/Yessir, the joint is jumpin'."

I read this first with my binoculars through the sliding glass door in my room. The door was stuck half-open, because the track was bent, and the sliding screen door behind was full of holes and tears. I covered them all with duct tape as best I could and lit two mosquito coils and placed them near the bed, hoping their smoke wouldn't set off the smoke alarm. I needn't have worried. The smoke alarm had no battery.

Here one could cross the border easily enough by paying the traditional five dollars, but foreigners could not, in these officious days, proceed to Kengtung. Even people from Thailand were being allowed only five kilometres inside Burma, and those from Burma (and Yunnan) only five kilometres inside Thailand. Yet the border opened at 0630 and closed at 1830, so I had many twelve-hour days investigating this most atypical piece of Burma, where the concrete shop-houses have two storeys above, rather than one, and are ornamented with enormous balustrades. I poked into every corner of all the shops, which sold military necessities, electronics smuggled from Singapore via Bangkok, gold, hardware, building materials, handicrafts, opium pipes, and surprisingly convincing antiques— just about everything that could be brought in, and out, legally or otherwise, and sold at a profit. Between times I hired pedicab drivers to take me through residential streets and back lanes at every time of day. Once, as I was putting my shoes back on after visiting a Buddhist shrine, I was approached by the abbot, an elderly man with a face the colour of a walnut husk, who not only spoke English but did so with the *r*'s of someone who had learned from native Britons, probably in England itself. He inquired in the most friendly way where I was from and what I was doing in his country. I said, truthfully, that I was bound eventually for Rangoon. "I am from Yangon," he replied with a trace of a smile or annoyance.

Like the border guards, drivers, shopkeepers, and almost everyone else I met in Tachilek, he placed great emphasis on asking what my profession was.

"Teacher," I said. Again, not a complete bare-faced lie. As soon as he asked that, I knew the abbot was probably corrupted, one of the hundreds of thousands of junta informers to be found on every block in every village, town, city, and rural district. No, I wasn't being paranoiac; I was simply in Burma. Burmophiles I know estimate that as many as one in three adult Burmans is an informant. Maybe *that's* paranoid. But we are discussing a poor country that spends more than forty percent of its gross national product on the military while half the children receive little or no education, where about nine percent of babies die in their first year. UNESCO statistics, all.

Only a short distance away from Mae Sai is the Golden Triangle. Not merely the metaphorical one for so long synonymous with the opium harvest and heroin production, nor even the broadly geographical Golden Triangle, an area of about a thousand square kilometres, but the actual Golden Triangle where the Sai River joins the mighty Mekong (locally Mae Klong) whose origins are in a bubbling spring in Tibet and whose mouth is below Saigon on the South China Sea. There is a actually a promontory where, once the morning mist has burned away, a person can stand in Thailand and look north towards China, a six-hour boat ride away, with Burma to the left and Laos to the right.

Everyone knows the opium trade is no longer centred there, however, and hasn't been since 1996 when Khun Sa, the leading opium warlord, surrendered to the Burmese junta and retired, or so most people believe. In any event, by that time the drug lords, whether those out for profit or others using the profits to support one political idealism or another, had discovered that crystal meth and other chemical drugs were less work and easier to transport. Which is not to say that the opium problem has disappeared. People who do well in chemical drugs help finance the Rangoon thugs as well as the dwindling bands of democrats and homeland seekers who resist the central government's authority. According to the English-language papers in Bangkok, one smuggler was killed and ten others, including two from Tachilek, had been arrested the previous weekend, bringing to forty-four the number charged in the past month alone with smuggling speed and heroin from Burma and Laos into Thailand. The very weekend I turned up at the Triangle another suspect was shot to death and fifteen more arrested with about one million Burmese-made pills, which were being moved from Chiang Rai to Chiang Mai for ultimate resale in Bangkok.

When I visited the Triangle, growers were about to start the traditional collection of seeds for next year's poppy crop, thus completing the cycle that begins with preparation of farming tools in March and April, continues through the clearing of fields by slash-and-burn in July and August, the broadcasting of seeds in September, the thinning of the young plants in October, the scoring to let the sap move freely, and the harvest itself in January and February when the bulbs are scraped with homemade crescent-shaped cleavers. The opium is formed into cakes and wrapped in paper. All of this is explained in detail at an opium museum on the summit overlooking the Mekong, a museum that is at once pro–Khun Sa and antidrug, for Khun Sa is, to say the least, a person whose memory lives on.

Within sight of the overlook there is a strange red building on the Burmese side of the river. This is a combination hotel and casino, stuck out in the jungle. The casino portion is open round the clock, but one wing of the hotel is still under construction a full decade after the groundbreaking. The delay is due to the fighting that breaks out periodically between the junta and the remnants of Khun Sa's force, now called the Mon Tai Army, led by Shan nationalists. After a long, careful climb down from the summit, I found the owner of a motorized dugout for hire, but he was reluctant to take me to the casino. His face betrayed a certain ambivalence, or maybe it was greed, unlike the Burmese officer on the road to Payathonzu. On the one hand, he knew I was trouble, knew the place I wanted to go to was trouble; on the other, I offered him cash. The second hand won out. He took me up river and pulled over to the casino's jetty, which was otherwise deserted. Leaving him there to protect his boat by fleeing, I was sure, at the first hint of trouble, I went inside, where my appearance made everyone's muscles go taut with hostility. What was apparent to me first of all was that this was not only a casino but also a bordello and second that it would never be a commercial success. Experienced capitalists would have followed the Las Vegas or Atlantic City model. They would have pushed through with construction of the hotel despite the rebels and so attracted Chinese who would stay overnight, stay in fact several nights or a week instead of only a few hours after the lengthy, uncomfortable trip from the Chinese border. Surely that's where the money is in casino gambling: wagering coated with profits from hospitality and entertainment. But this casino and whorehouse was owned and run by members of the Burmese military who, being both communists and capitalists, are skilled at neither. I stayed as long as seemed prudent and was relieved to see the skittish boatman hadn't left without me. But then I hadn't given him the right-hand half of his paper money in advance. He had to remain at the jetty and return me to my point of origin to get paid at all. I was either wising up or getting dumber, I wasn't sure which.

The day before I arrived in the area the Bangkok papers had carried news of a drug bust in the Triangle involving a caravan of opium and pills, for this was during or just after harvest time, with all its traditional festivals and gunplay. In fact, opium-growing has been a local activity going back to antiquity among the indigenous peoples in particular, each of which has its own traditional implements and instruments. Take the matter of opium scales. The Chinese style folds into a case that looks like a wooden fan, while the Akha, who still partake of the pipe in the villages near by, have metal ones that resemble the scales of justice in the statue atop the Old Bailey in London. So too with pipes. Some are jade, others silver or porcelain or clay. In ancient China they were terra-cotta. And weights for measuring. Some are ceramic, others bronze or brass; some are made from moulds using beeswax, a commodity still sold in all local markets. Some weights take on craft or artistic importance. The most interesting ones depict the twelve animals representing the years in the Chinese lunar calendar.

Khun Sa, while posing as a Shan freedom fighter, was a scumbag who showed his ultimate contempt for humanity by selling out to Rangoon. Until then he was just a criminal with a private army and vast interests in smuggled teak, jade, and gems as well as dope, an independent criminal, unsanctioned by the junta. Yet he wasn't always a lone wolf, and his personal vitae are worth reciting, because they are the story of the region in recent times. Khun Sa, also known as Chang Xi Fu, had one Shan parent and one Chinese. He joined Ne Win's forces early and by 1963 was a colonel in the all-important intelligence division. In 1966 he was ordered to accompany transport caravans carrying sixty thousand kilograms of dope. One was going from Burma via Mae Sai and the other to Ban Kwan in Laos. In those days, and as recently as the 1990s, mules were used to pack drugs over the mountains. As the Americans learned during the Second World War, mules were the only effective means of transport in such country; the last mules and muleteers weren't phased out of the US military until 1956 when helicopters solved the problem of rugged terrain. In any event, both caravans were captured, the first by Burmese renegades, the other by Chinese. Khun Sa was taken prisoner along with them. He was quite a prize. The junta took two Russian doctors prisoner who were traded for his release, whereupon he joined the Shan United Army and went into business for himself as a criminal executive and local folk hero.

At Chiang Saen, near the Thai point of the Triangle, lies a small jetty with some long-tail boats for hire, as well as bigger local vessels. I engaged one of the former to take me up the Mekong to a point where I could enter Laos without much fuss. Even during the dry season, the Mekong is a mighty river, a kilometre wide it seemed to me and, in the centre channel, maybe ten or twelve metres deep, or so I was told. It's swift and cold and the colour of muddy tea. When I dipped my hands in it, I felt connected to an ancient world.

One of the hill tribes of northern Thailand, the Hmong, originates in Laos. During the Vietnam War, these particular ones allied themselves with the side that lost, only to be deserted by the CIA and the Pentagon after aiding them in their campaign. Those who could, fled to America. One of the largest Hmong colonies is in Minneapolis, of all places; others are in San Diego and Fresno. Those who couldn't, escaped into Thailand. Some of them are still fighting a ragtag, hit-and-run resistance to the communist regime that took over in Vientiane in 1975, the same year the Americans were driven out of Vietnam. Since then Laos has remained a mysterious country for the most part. Not scary like Burma. Passive-aggressive rather than paranoiac. Parts of it, especially on the other side, along the border shared with the former North Vietnam, remain obscure. In 1992 outside experts for the first time stumbled on a deerlike mammal called the saola, or Vu Quang ox, after the area of the same name. As recently as 1997, a species of wild pig previously unknown to science was observed in Laos. Even along the Mekong, the great highway of the region with its Chinese riverboats and solitary fishers, Laos seems odd. The near-constant mist contributes to the feeling, but there is more to it than that.

Passing several fishing villages, where ingress was known to be bureaucratically difficult, we came at last to the one we sought. Its main picturesque attraction was a tea house and shop featuring a table with three large jars of whisky. Floating in one was the carcass of a big lizard. Coiled up in the second was a snake, resembling the coral snakes of North America. In the third were the penis and testicles of a Laotian tiger. A stack of glasses was nearby. Elderly males seeking to renew their sexual vigour pay by the glass for the whisky of their choice. Showing greater curiosity than good sense, I had a shot of the tiger juice. It tasted like moonshine that had gone off, but I suffered no ill effects in the days ahead. No beneficial ones either.

There was one more place I wanted to go before biting the bullet and using up my precious one-month Burmese visa: Mae Hong Son, the combination trekkers' haven and smugglers' town on the western (wild western) border. This is in Shan territory, but several other tribal peoples are scattered about, including the Karen, who were the object of my interest. The largest concentration of Karen refugees was the fifteen thousand at Ban Mae Kong Kha, who help in illegal teak logging, for the benefit of—whom? Which government, which warlord, which ethnic group lies at the back of each such scheme or dodge is a complicated matter indeed. I had no hope of getting into Ban Mae Kong Kha, as the Thai Seventh Infantry had sealed it off completely in the wake of recent events. But there were any number of smaller encampments, village size, nearby. Indeed *refugee villages* is a more precise term, as the people in them, a hundred here, a hundred and fifty there, have to fend for themselves. The Thais keep the Burmese from attacking them by incursion (though they couldn't prevent the odd rocket bombardment from within Burma), but they provided no supplies or aid as far as I knew. Refugees were still crossing into Thai territory, since fighting was going on only a kilometre or two inside Burma.

Getting where I wanted to go took eleven or twelve hours, retracing my steps back through Chiang Rai south to Chiang Mai, then west to Mae Hong Son. I was beginning to feel that wherever I wished to go in Thailand took twelve hours. The last portion of the trip was wild: a crazy ride on a local bus from Chiang Mai that flew along-side range after range of mountains on one of the most precipitous and certainly one of the most dangerous roads I had ever experienced, which first had been pushed through by the Japanese during the Second World War. It was dark when I reached Mae Hong Son intact. The principal street was full of guest houses and small hotels, the kinds of places that cater to trekkies, not to Chinese celebrating the lunar new year. Accordingly I found a room for the night with no difficulty. As is the custom in cheap Thai hotels now, on checking in I was issued a thin hand towel (no facecloth), a little bar of soap, and two condoms, even though I was clearly alone. Condoms are called raincoats in Thai slang.

At six the next morning I met a young woman of mixed Thai

and Indian descent. Her name was Midori. She was, I gathered, a student activist. Through a one-in-a-million shot she was headed for the same area I was, but for a different reason. She was doing an informal study of the Padaung women. The Padaung, who live west of the Salween River in the area that takes in parts of both Kayah State and Karen State, are famous in the outside world because of the so-called long-neck women, who still follow the custom of seeming to stretch their necks by wearing brass coils. (Actually they're not stretching their necks but pushing down their collarbones.) Instinct told me Midori could be trusted. She must have felt the same about me. Either that or she was a pretty good actor. In any event, as we were travelling in the same general direction but with different motives, we decided to meet up the following morning and proceed together, sharing expenses and a long-tail boat.

This is one of the most interesting parts of Thailand, the setting of one of the great unwritten stories of the Chinese Revolution. When Chiang Kai-shek and the Kuomintang fled the Mainland for Formosa in 1949, several KMT divisions in Yunnan and the far south were cut off. They fought the communists in some cases until well into the 1960s. But mostly they settled in Thailand and supported themselves through various illegal activities. There are still KMT settlements, with third-generation KMT descendants, though few if any of the original soldiers can have survived after all these decades. If any do, they persist in Galápagos-like isolation from the rest of the Republic of China, for Taiwan has long since reformed and embraced democracy, though at this time the KMT was still the dominant political party.

The boatman took Midori and me along a tributary of the Salween (sometimes, Salawin). He travelled at a high rate of speed despite water so low there were many shoals and rapids and passages along the way so labyrinthine that people had erected cairns to indicate which side of the islands to follow. Twice along the way we saw elephants working in the bush. The boatmen knew well how to find the Padaung, and we spent the first day following Midori's agenda, calling at one of their villages, where I was surprised to see that the women made Shan shoulder bags, the sort one sees all over Burma but which I somehow had assumed were a Shan monopoly. She, I, and the boatman spent the night in the village.

I confess I passed out early from fatigue but was therefore up all the earlier in the morning, raring to get under way, farther up the tortuous river and its various branches. Before long we caught a glimpse of a Karen thatched roof, indicating a village, but one that was considered off-limits and "unsafe" at the moment, because of the continuing aftermath of hostage-takings and executions. The boatman said the village was guarded by a few Burmese soldiers, though we didn't see them. He said the same of another village later. Finally we came to the oldest Karen refugee community in the area. I got the boatman to see if there was a headman about. It seemed unlikely, for there were no males in sight—no Burmese but no Karen either. They were presumably off fighting or working, leaving behind the women and children. My guess was they were fighting or, being known as fighters, had been captured and put to slave labour. Because of the low water, some of the village, normally a Thai island, was now actually located on Burmese soil. With what pleasure I walked over the gravel into Burma without any hindrance, without the Burmese even being round to snoop, and spent a couple of hours writing in my journal, my bottom firmly planted in Burma where I wasn't supposed to be.

I was right about there being a headman left behind, not an elderly fellow, as I had expected, but younger than I: an increasingly common phenomenon. He spoke Thai and so Midori was able to translate for me. I told the headman how much I admired Karen perseverance, that I was sad to see their resistance weakening, that they must not lose their resolve against the thugs in Rangoon. Midori translated this a little uneasily, but I could tell by the headman's face and eyes that the message was getting through. What I most wanted to say was: "Hold on, hold on. Help is coming from the West." But I couldn't because it's not true and never will be true. I couldn't even tell him that the plight of his people is well-known in the West when in fact the West is blinded by the sight of China, which it continues to see with candy-store eyes as one vast market for corporate America.

I opened my backpack and gave the headman anything I could live without that I thought might be useful to his village or the men in the field: a canteen, an extra pair of jeans, my elaborate medical kit complete with sutures and even scalpels, my compass on a lanyard, toiletries and soap, my mosquito net, pens and paper, my emergency supply of freeze-dried food, and my energy bars for blood-sugar lows. I also gave him all the baht I had and the few American dollars I could spare.

Even though the boatman was being paid by the hour, he didn't seem eager for us to linger any longer. As he, Midori, and I clambered awkwardly back to the boat, Midori said to me, "You have earned merit."

"I need all the merit I can get," I replied.

IRRAWADDY HIGHWAY

*T*he time had come for me to stop snooping along the border, sneaking across when no one was looking, and to use my precious Burmese visa. The time had come to cross legally so that I could get to Rangoon, Pagan (which the junta calls Bagan), and Mandalay (which unaccountably is still known by the same name as in colonial days). These are located on the broad Irrawaddy (in newspeak Ayeyarwady) or rather, in Rangoon's case, on the incredibly wide and complex delta through which the river system feeds the Gulf of Martaban, the Bay of Bengal, the Andaman Sea, and ultimately the Indian Ocean. The type of visa I could get with the minimum (but still rather substantial amount) of trouble, without arousing my unfair share of suspicion, was as part of a group tour. Two months aboard the ship from Athens to Tahiti had made my horror of group travel permanent, so I chose to join a band of predominantly German-speaking tourists for a passage upriver. As I understand or speak no German, I was in little danger of being conversed with. I figured out that once safely inside Burma with my German friends I could easily go AWOL and wander off on my own, returning just in time for the various head counts and bed checks. That was the plan anyway.

There were ten or twelve of us. We all had confirmed seats on a Thai flight from Bangkok. At the last moment the Burmese, with their customary ambivalence about admitting foreigners, an ambivalence matched by foreigners' reluctance to visit, refused to honour the visas unless we switched to the state-owned Myanmar Air, whose two-letter code is still UB, for Union of Burma, the nation's pre-junta name. The short flight was made confusing by the fact that Burma perversely declares itself one half hour farther ahead of GMT than Thailand does; in this respect it is the Newfoundland of Asia. Myanmar Air was like a miniature Aeroflot, but the view of the delta was spectacular, with hundreds of muddy fingers spread out below in patterns that seemed impossibly complex from thirty thousand feet and must be truly labyrinthine at sea level. As soon as we arrived at the terminal, we were given the latest issue of the shopping magazine *Beauty of Myanmar,* which sets the tone on the front page:

People's Desire
Oppose those relying on external elements, acting as stooges, holding negative views.
Oppose those trying to jeopardize stability of the State and progress of the nation.
Oppose foreign nations interfering in internal affairs of the State.
Crush all internal and external destructive elements as the common enemy.

This same mission statement is published every day in the *New Light of Myanmar,* surely one of the most wretched English-language newspapers on which the late 1st Baron Thomson never got his hands. The remainder of *Beauty of Myanmar* is taken up with a curious mixture of shipping ads, propaganda, and statistical disinformation. For example, a table shows foreign tourism rising steadily to a record of one hundred and seventeen thousand four hundred and ninety visitors in 1998, with Japan and Taiwan together accounting for nearly fifty thousand. More than one other source holds that tourism has been flatlined for the past couple of years at about fifty thousand visitors total.

One of the reasons for wishing to flee my base camp in Bangkok at this time was that the city was filling with police and military at an alarming rate. This had been the general trend since the shoot-out at Ratchaburi. The process was really picking up speed now on the eve of the quadrennial United Nations Conference on Trade and Development, which was bringing one hundred and ninety world leaders to the city for two weeks. In the present unsettled atmosphere along the border, Thai authorities feared, at the least, a repeat of the anti-globalization protests that had distinguished the recent World Trade Organization talks in Seattle. Authority figures, from troops in Kevlar helmets to business-suited security officers talking into their cufflinks, were in every hotel lobby and public building—everywhere. Groups of women wearing cotton carapaces and large straw hats were descending the sewer systems on ropes to check for bombs before the manhole covers were welded shut. Police divers were scouring the bottom of the river. Foreigners were being watched closely, and in some cases rounded up for questioning. I would make myself scarce by going to Rangoon, though it was of course impossible to make myself inconspicuous there, even though I had a local contact. Out of concern for her safety I'll call her M.

We hadn't met before, but we knew each other to be, generally speaking, on the same side. Still, I was impressed with the way she generously talked with me about politics, even though we were careful where these discussions took place, as talking to foreigners about Burmese politics is another crime. But then so is an unauthorized conversation involving five or more Burmese citizens congregated in a public place. So is having access to information from the West, at least if one isn't part of the strange little parallel universe of joint-venture companies and American-dollar foreigners. For example, foreign firms in Burma, which have grown more common since the junta abandoned any pretence of true socialism while tightening its death grip on the people, are free to use fax machines and computers. Such technology was out of the reach of individual non-affiliated

Burmese, first by statute, now by the more effective means of limiting them to people with easy access to US dollars. Even so, the government found it necessary, just before my visit, as it happened, to shut down the last two Internet service providers doing business with Burmese civilians, lest corrupting information about the outside world slip between the slats. Many international companies now fiddle their e-mail accounts by using jitneys in Singapore.

As a country that is under martial law, Burma naturally has a curfew, though like many of the laws it is applied with varying degrees of strictness in various provinces and even from one county to another. Of course, the strongest argument against being abroad at night is the danger from mosquitoes. Most Burmese sleep under nets. Perhaps partly as a result, malaria is actually only the third most prevalent deadly disease after tuberculosis and AIDS. Several years ago there were stories in the West that the junta was keeping its statistics low by the method of injecting HIV patients with potassium cyanide. Later information led even the western human-rights groups with a special interest in Burma to deny this, at least insofar as any deliberate policy was concerned, as distinct perhaps from some isolated instance in the past. Incidentally Burma is one of the few countries that still has a leper colony, though its population is now miniscule. Other crimes at present include having a photograph of Suu Kyi on the wall of one's home, though such an image is much more likely to be noticed in the city than in the countryside. As an expatriate actor says in John Boorman's film *Beyond Rangoon,* "In Burma everything is illegal." Sometimes it certainly seems that way. During the course of a given year, a hundred citizens of Mandalay are sent to jail for not observing the zebra crossings: apparently a different and more heinous crime than simple jaywalking or failing to use the pedestrian overpasses. Naturally there isn't even a semblance of a free press, and the junta strictly controls television, most efficiently by forcing people to rely on satellite dishes, which it makes certain they can never afford. As a result, Burmese know little, other than what they're fed, about what's going on in their country, much less elsewhere. People they know may disappear, particularly into the scary-looking Insein prison, most notorious of all the political torture chambers. The citizenry in general, however, seems to have no comprehension of slave labour, including the porterage on the Thai frontier and the scale on which it is practised by the Tatmadaw. Nor do they seem fully aware of the slow and sure war of expulsion, enslavement, and extermination being waged against the hill tribes.

One day in Rangoon, M and I were walking to Inya Lake, about twenty minutes equidistant from the airport to the north and the central city to the south. It is a lovely island-studded lake in the northern part of the city, fringed by gardens and bamboo groves. M wasn't being overtly political—I felt she knew she didn't have to convince me—but kept making offhand remarks that seemed to betray where she stood.

"Over there, on the left-hand side of the road, are the Zoological Gardens," she said. "All of that on the right-hand side is part of Tatmadaw. Notice, please, that they both have high fences with spikes on the top. I have wondered whether these are for keeping their animals inside or keeping us animals out."

She was tiny, with the textbook features and complexion of the ethnic Burman of the lowlands. She wore a stiff white cotton blouse and a longyi. Like all Burmese, female and male, she stopped every half hour or so to readjust the longyi round her waist and retie it. Women's longyis, which are a solid colour or perhaps in a floral pattern, are knotted once, on the side; men's, which are usually checked or plaid, tie twice and knot in the front. M's had a bird motif. She had one of those little voices, like Jackie Kennedy's, but with more of a singsong quality. She used graceful hand gestures when she spoke.

"That road leads to the Lady's house," she said as we neared University Avenue. She said "the Lady" for Aung Sang Suu Kyi the way a taxi driver in Chile had said "the Guy" when speaking of Augusto Pinochet: these two figures may be political opposites, but in their different ways their names were dangerous to say aloud. Two soldiers were posted at the turnoff, but they didn't appear to be part of an official checkpoint. M spoke ever more softly, though no one could overhear us.

"This is as far as they permit you to go, even after her release from house arrest." Then she lowered her voice to just a whisper. "But I have been there."

The Lady's house is across the lake from, but not actually in sight of, the compound where the elderly Ne Win, the man who had her father assassinated and set the stage for the junta, lives, surrounded by his fellow paranoiacs and his geomancers, still secretly plotting (many believe) the course of Burmese politics, even now, two long generations after the original coup and several years after the dreaded SLORC handed power to a younger group of officers and became the SPDC instead. Yet despite her contacts with the Lady, M suffered from lack of information about what was going on in her country. For example, the raid by God's Army on the hospital at Ratchaburi and the subsequent counterattack by the Thai military were events of major international significance, permanently affecting the politics of Burma and Thailand and indeed the entire region. M was aware of the occurrence only by chance, having overheard two tourists who had been following the events on CNN, where this had been the lead story for two or three consecutive days. She had to depend on me for the details and news of the repercussions.

As I got to know M, I learned several contradictory and some- times disturbing facts about her and her family. Her father was a career military officer who had been pushed aside by SLORC and then ran for a parliamentary seat in the notorious 1990 election as a candidate of the National League for Democracy. As a result, he served a stretch in prison. M read me some of his letters, which were brave and heartbreaking. But his sentence was relatively short, about eighteen months, because many of his old classmates from military school were able to help him. Once free, however, he didn't join the government-in-exile in the United States, unlike so many of the others who had won and were denied their seats. He stayed put and kept his head down. M's mother was a gem dealer by profession, selling from her home to ten or so select clients the stones she got either from the far north, above Mandalay, or from contacts among the Chin on the Indian border who, in the Indian fashion, preferred to hoard gold, which she bartered with them. Like most such businesses in Burma, this was a matrilineal one, passed from grandmother to mother to daughter. But M had rejected it, even after (and because) she graduated from Rangoon University with a first in English language and literature shortly before the campuses were shut down by the military.

"As a result of the closing of the universities," she said, "there is one generation of people without the education to take up their rightful positions as doctors, engineers, and so on." As for herself, she spent her time as a translator and tutor, working from the family home. She had studied George Eliot and the Brontës like the rest of us but had never set foot outside Burma, not even in Laos or India or China, and certainly never in so western a place as Thailand, and seemed unlikely to do so unless the politics changed dramatically. "A couple of years ago I joined one of the International Red Cross agencies that help refugees," she said. "The government cancelled my passport." To the Burmese government the Red Cross looks like another subversive western terrorist band, and it now probably feels so even more strongly, given that the Red Cross has had some success in visiting the prisons and observing conditions there.

I felt guilty about taking her time, but she said she had "much time and little to do—in fact, I've had little to do for nearly fifteen years, except to study the teaching of the Buddha." She refused to accept any money from anyone for her own use, on any pretext. "It is good for me to be able to spend so much time with a native speaker of English, even one whose English is as strange as your own," she said with no humour or sarcasm whatsoever in her voice or intent.

We decided to continue our talks as we moved through the city, where we were pretty careful to stick to the obvious touristy spots, as there seemed little doubt, what with who she was and who I must have appeared to be, that we were being followed.

Accordingly she took me to the Shwedagon Pagoda, the most important Buddhist shrine in the country and Rangoon's principal landmark. It is built atop a golden vault said to contain three hairs from the head of Buddha. Marco Polo recorded that the gold covering the conical spire of the main temple in the complex was the thickness of a person's finger. Such may well be true in spots, though now the preferred material is gold leaf, whose manufacturing, by means of endless hammering, is a famous local craft. The Shwemawdaw Pagoda at Bago (or Pegu), about a hundred and forty kilometres northeast, is taller than the main temple at Shwedagon but can hardly be more impressive. The prefix *shwe* means gold, and Shwedagon, sitting at the centre of a vast city of lesser shrines and chedis, was said by the British, who used it as a military stronghold, to contain more gold than the vaults beneath the Bank of England. Hardly true, of course, especially in those days, but certainly tonnes of gold were involved, as well as rubies and other precious gems on the spire. I enjoyed thinking the person or persons tailing us couldn't be certain if they were following Fetherling the student of religious architecture or Fetherling the gemologist.

Of course, the point of Shwedagon is not its wealth but rather what the wealth was used to honour. Money for the pagodas has been donated entirely by individuals over twelve centuries (twenty-five, if you believe the folklore). Even today many rural people, the very ones least able to afford to do so, give thirty percent of their earnings to support their local temple. Devotion on that scale is harder to find among the urban population (and one Burmese in ten lives in Rangoon). Looking only at Shwedagon, however, makes it difficult for an outsider to imagine that any diminishing of devoutness is taking place. All Burmese Buddhists know on what day of the week they were born and say prayers at the station of Shwedagon that matches. For astrological reasons, however, there are eight such stations, meaning that, for religious purposes, there must be eight days to the week as well; the answer is to have two Wednesdays—Low Wednesday and High Wednesday. The people come to the outer perimeter of the main pagoda, round which, evenly spaced, are wooden poles denoting the eight days. Standing or kneeling at the appropriate spot, they throw water and make other offerings. A stranger could easily get lost in this astounding maze of architecture. Certainly I would have done so if I hadn't been accompanied by M.

The small shops selling what she called "religious auxiliaries" reminded me in some ways of the Mingalar and Htedan markets, where Rangoon shops for its food and clothing. Everything else— yes, virtually everything else—may be bought from one of the two thousand stalls of the Bogyoke Aung San Market, still known to many by its old colonial name, Scott Market. But then I was surprised to see just how much of British Rangoon survives in the city centre. For example, the government ministries building where Aung San was assassinated in 1948 is still the government ministries building. Similarly the redbrick law courts, with their characteristically British clock tower visible at a great distance, are still the law courts.

The area for a couple of blocks round the law courts is the traditional home to stationers and booksellers, whose businesses, like so many in Asia generally and perhaps Burma in particular, are conducted partly out on the pavement. I spent the better part of a day browsing the shops in detail, discovering that perhaps five or ten percent of the books are in English and that hardly any are new, except for copies of George Orwell's *Burmese Days,* which is everywhere. No doubt the junta approves of its depiction of British imperialism. Of course, there are no copies of *Animal Farm* or *Nineteen Eighty-Four. Burmese Days* is available in two editions: the genuine Penguin and the pirated Penguin. Overall, the available English-language books are overwhelmingly ones on how to learn English—dictionaries, grammars, spellers, primers. "This is because people like to make money," M told me later. "In the Burmese language we have scores of words for what you just call *love* in English. But the people all want to learn English, which is mostly a business language." As though to prove her point, the next most common category of English book includes anything pertaining to some commercial or technological subject. Many of them are a half century old, left behind in a hurry at Independence; many have since been carefully resewn into paper covers made of something very much like what we used to call butcher's paper. There are virtually no books on computers and precious little literature except for a few novels of the Somerset Maugham or J. B. Priestley type.

Because of this new strength of the English language, and the popular demand with which it has been greeted, Rangoon seemed a more polyglot place than it actually is. Without its Chinatown and Little India, which add most of the bustle to the streets, the city would be more colourful than kinetic. A statistic I find difficult to believe, but one I kept running across in source after source, is that the total number of expats living in Burma, including embassy personnel, is only five hundred. And moreover that Koreans are the largest single group. As they are in every Asian city, European visitors are carefully shown the Catholic church, the Protestant church, and the mosque as well as either the Buddhist or the Hindu temples, in order to prove that religious tolerance is a policy. Having stumbled on all of these in my wandering, I asked if there was also a synagogue, for a Jewish community is always a sign of true rather than artificial cosmopolitanism and freedom. Oh yes indeed, I was told. And one may visit it openly. Of course, it is, sadly, no longer used as a place of worship as the total Jewish population of Rangoon, child and adult, male and female, has shrunk to only thirty-five. Among them, evidently, a minyan cannot be found.

Rangoon is a poor city but full of bustle despite the heat (forty degrees Celsius when I was there a few weeks before the hot season was due to begin). Everyone makes something, or at least sells something. Outdoor cobblers are almost as common as outdoor seamstresses, with their tiny foot-powered sewing machines, or street-corner barbers. These providers of services exist cheek-by-jowl with the craftspeople, such as those who make the lacquered marionettes of which the Burmese are so fond, ones depicting mythological creatures or folk-loric figures such as the *zawgti*, a kind of red-robed magician and superhero. Some entrepreneurs, down by the river especially, save their money to buy three or even four packs of cigarettes, all of dif-ferent brands, then sit on the curb selling them one cigarette at a time—a common enough sight anywhere in the developing world, of course. In Rangoon, however, I saw more than one street-corner merchant whose merchandise consisted solely of toothpicks. They were done up in little bundles and looked like miniature versions of firewood that one sees people buying in small faggots—just enough for a day's cooking. How many toothpicks must a man (they were always men) sell in a day to keep his family in rice? Recently a fellow Burmophile told me he once saw a Rangoon sidewalk seller whose goods consisted entirely of the unsorted insides of an old alarm clock.

Despite the neat British street grid, Rangoon is a chaotic city. It is chaotic partly because in the inevitable fit of nationalistic pride following Independence, the Burmese decided to stop driving on the left like their former masters and drive on the right. This was less a problem when automobiles were less common, though it's always been a nuisance when crossing to or from neighbouring Thailand, for the Thais were never a western colony and attach no political sig-nificance to driving on the same side as the Japanese who manufacture their cars. The Burmese aren't rich enough to constitute a market like America, for which the Japanese, of course, build cars for right-lane driving. In fact, all the Burmese can afford to import is secondhand Japanese cars built originally for domestic Japanese consumption. So Burmese motorists sit on the right side of the seat while driving in the left lane, putting themselves and others in untold danger, especially at intersections and roundabouts. Passing is particularly dangerous. Car crashes are more common than coughs. People walk round with their arms in slings without provoking comment or inquiry. I was put in mind of Jean-Luc Godard's film *Weekend* in which there is one long highway accident that appears to go on forever.

There is no mass public transit, only a system of small Japanese vans in which monks ride on top, women and children sit on benches inside and men hang on to the sides; men and women pay the same fare, but monks ride free. These vehicles frequently break down, and it is common to see the secular male passengers assisting in the repairs while the monks sit back aloofly, sometimes smoking cigarettes. I saw one group of commuters debating what to do with the carburetor they had dismantled on the spot. (I couldn't bear to watch. Carburetors look too much like human hearts.) In addition, there are still a few large wooden-sided buses from the Second World War era, kept on the road by nothing more than a level of mechanical skill that even the Cubans might admire. All this transportation is taking place amid constant noise, including government propaganda broadcast in the streets and the cackling babble of police loudhailers. And there seems to be a different smell round each corner, whether of fish heads or incense or simply the universal odour of poverty.

Rangoon is also, supremely, a city of soldiers—plain and fancy, old and young, urban and rural, well armed and unarmed. One sees them in military vehicles of every description as well as on bicycles. Most statistics on the Burmese military are a generation out-of-date, so estimates of its size vary wildly. The higher-end guesses give it a standing army of about six hundred and fifty thousand. Given that thirty-four percent of the population is under fifteen (the age of enlistment) and that more than half of the remainder are women (who may not join) and a certain percentage are elderly, this suggests six hundred and fifty thousand troops from a pool of about twelve and a half million. The force is an entirely voluntary one. It needn't be otherwise, as so many see the army as their best opportunity to get enough to eat. Military installations and businesses are everywhere.

"This is an expensive residential district," M said, gesturing to what was obviously, well, an expensive residential district. We were walking through the north-central part of the city. "Here live the generals and the other people in the drug business." I wasn't able to gauge the level of her irony, but I don't believe it was high. Of course, not everyone joins the army to share the booty. Many join out of patriotism. Some others out of respect for the Spartan life; this is especially true perhaps of the younger soldiers, those who already have had some taste of discipline from having served briefly as novice monks, as males are required to do for a time. A disproportionate number of the younger soldiers are from rural areas.

Frankly I was unable to tell one soldier from another, sometimes to the point of not being able to distinguish officers from other ranks. This was frustrating because one of the missions I had assigned myself was to collect as many impressions of the military as I could safely gather. Pay attention to their boots, I had told myself before leaving home: a well-shod army is one that's being looked after, one that's most likely to fight. But what can you make of any army where some men are in spit-polished paratrooper boots and others wear flip-flops? I spent a day at the army museum, which is open to the public, though the appearance there of any visitor, much less a foreign one, seems to trigger the guards' suspicion. At least I came away knowing how to distinguish a member of Northern Command from a member of Southern, indeed how to identify a sapper from a transport man, which is more than I knew when I started, more in fact than I had been able to learn from the various *Jane's* military publications. The process was somewhat analogous to my unsuccessful struggles with the basics of the Burmese language. I had been reduced to finding words in a phrasebook and pointing them out to bewildered pedicab drivers. Before the journey started I searched the Internet diligently, trying to locate some teach-yourself-elementary-Burmese audiotapes. I could locate only one set on the market. It was frightfully expensive and also, I learned when it arrived in the post two months later, totally useless. It consisted of tapes made from scratchy old vinyl disks circa 1947. The little exercises consisted of a British voice with crystal vowels saying such things as "Instruct the boy to fetch the motorcar." With great perseverance I might have been able to handle the servants but not ask where the toilet was.

My days in Rangoon were growing short as I had passage on a river ferry to Pagan (Bagan), the quiet holy place of antiquity, three days upriver, where I could catch a better class of boat to Mandalay, a day or two farther along. The night before, I said goodbye to M, though reluctantly, and was surprised—the word is scarcely adequate—to find a note from her slipped under my hotel door the next morning. I was up at 0500, so she must have come by in the middle of the night, curfew be damned. Her handwriting was fascinating—English letters with Burmese dots and ligatures—and so was her choice of words. Her written vocabulary was nowhere near so impressive as her spoken, but she certainly communicated well enough to shock me. She told me she'd fallen in love with me and couldn't live without me. This isn't the type of letter I receive often, or ever; you have to know me to appreciate how farfetched, even intrinsically preposterous, such a proposition is. I began to think she was an informer, not the democrat she claimed. Fuck. A spy had been leading me round by the nose.

After first shouldering my backpack and settling my bill, I spent the morning wandering where I hoped she wouldn't find me (unless she was working in concert with the intelligence thugs who had tailed us, which didn't seem unlikely somehow). When the hour was right, I started walking southward towards the high bank that keeps the river from the city's view. The last street before one leaves Rangoon behind is the Strand. Not only has it retained its British name, but the government has permitted Dutch investors to revitalize its most famous landmark, the eponymous Strand Hotel, built in 1896 by the same people who owned the E&O in Penang. Now the Strand, located immediately in front of the police intelligence headquarters, is no E&O, though it is tony. Because it was closed for so long and neglected for longer still, the Dutch had a fairly simple time restoring it to a condition approximating its former colonial self-assurance. Yes, there are teak-bladed ceiling fans revolving slowly. Yes, there is a dress code (I just squeaked by). Yes, Joseph Conrad would have stayed there. Feeling a debt to history, I entered the bar, deserted in the early afternoon, and ordered a G&T with Bombay Sapphire, as I thought Clio over my shoulder would have demanded. While I waited I was asked to browse through a bound copy of the *Rangoon Times* Special Christmas Number for 1912.

The ferry was stubby, like the old Japanese railway carriages you sometimes catch glimpses of both in Burma and Thailand, had three decks, and had been painted white throughout, the way one paints one's first apartment. I found it berthed among vessels of various descriptions, all either embarking or disembarking and filled with passengers or goods, many of them carrying on the trade Burma engages in with all its neighbours except Laos (as the two countries are rich and poor in the same commodities, such trade is pointless). Burma doesn't manufacture much, just some paint and other simple chemical products. The era when it was the world's leading exporter of rice is far behind. The population has trebled since then and agricultural methods haven't kept up: twelve million cattle are still used in Burmese farming, but few tractors, not even secondhand ones. By contrast it imports expensive electronics from Singapore and Japan and equally costly pharmaceuticals, such as an antimalarial called Dihydroatremisin, from China. I bought some Burmese sticky rice, which comes in baskets with lids that look like miniatures of the packs used to haul opium. It tastes much different from the Chinese varieties wrapped in leaves; stickier for one thing and a little sweet. Traditionally it is eaten with only the fingers, specifically the fingers of the right hand.

Getting from the Rangoon River to the Irrawaddy through the canal that connects them was over before I realized what we were doing. Rangoon is a tightly packed city and, by Burmese standards, a high-density one (there are seven-storey buildings). But because it was never a highly industrialized one, not even under the British, the outskirts aren't surrounded by rusty manufacturing capacity. The city is decorated with green spaces, then there are a few modern suburbs, and then other green areas, unplanned ones, become dominant and the city fades away. I was mopping my brow in the land of the town people, and the next I knew we were in the realm of the river folk: fishers who work two to a boat, casting their nets in a wide fan again and again, dawn to sunset, and the transporters who carry commodities and passengers up and down the river, which looked light blue in the distance but was brown up close. Continually I was told the river is still the main artery of transport, even though it is by no means so busy as it was, now that a north-south highway has opened. It's still busy enough in any event to be reminiscent of an earlier era, both in Burma and elsewhere.

We passed many little towns, from our vantage point mere indentations in the landscape: Nyaungdon, Danubyu, Hinthada, Shegyin, Kanaung, Htonbo, Sinte. The river seemed impossibly wide, even though this was the dry season when huge sandbars, some of them large enough to be called desert islands, lay exposed to provide space for fishers' lean-to colonies. Although the current was swift, we saw few sawyers or other dangerous debris. The ever-shifting sandbars, however, showed why the ferries were built as they are, with hulls in the same basic shape as tablespoons. Sometimes the captain found it necessary to take on a local pilot, who knew the present conditions—namely, where the channel was among all the false indications. Such pilots stayed aboard for only a few kilometres, the territory they knew best. At its deepest the river was six metres or more. Our draught was a mere one and a half metres. Yet to keep from going aground required a man posted at the prow with a long bamboo pole, painted in alternating yellow and black bands, each exactly one foot wide. He would continually shout out the depth at the top of his lungs to a fellow sailor immediately behind, squatting over the lazaret, who would relay the shout to the engine room by means of a small bronze bell. Mark Twain would have recognized the procedure in an instant. Avoiding accident also meant we followed a zigzag course upstream until the last bit of light was extinguished and we were forced to tie up for the night.

As we shifted towards first one bank and then the other, avoiding the ripples and following the deepest soundings, so did the Irrawaddy do a slow dance this direction and that until in time we came to the first important city, Pyay, formerly Prome, which lies just a bit south of Srishetra, one of the many cities (I counted thirteen) to have served as capital of the Burmese state or its old dynastic predecessors. Pyay's High Street isn't actually the High Street. That honour belongs to the Strand. Such touches are a reminiscence of Pyay's importance in colonial times, as this was one of the major stops in that wonderfully named enterprise, the Irrawaddy Flotilla and Burmese Steam Navigation Company Limited, the IF for short, "the old Flotilla" of Kipling's "Road to Mandalay." This fleet of steamers and cargo flats was a Glasgow concern that grew even larger as the British, seeking profit and fearing incursions by the French, slowly gained control of more and more of the river until they dominated all navigable portions. In its heyday the Flotilla had steamers of ninety metres, a third longer than any craft on the river today, and could cram in as many as four thousand passengers, most of them on deck, of course.

When the Japanese invaded Burma during the Second World War, the fleet, then six hundred and fifty strong, was positioned so as to create obstruction and then scuttled. In some cases employees sank the boats by piercing their thin metal hulls with Bren gun fire. The Japanese were thus denied use of the fleet and faced a major hazard to navigation. After the war, the shell of the company was nationalized by the Burmese government. Even a few of the hulls were raised and rebuilt. Today the much smaller state-owned river fleet still uses the black-and-red livery of the old Flotilla. We passed at least one of these vessels on this part of the river while I was conscious. It wasn't crowded or very impressive. I didn't have a detailed map of the Irrawaddy to confirm this (large-scale maps of Burma are hard to come by, being by their nature subversive), but my impression was that between Pyay and Pagan, one day farther upstream, the river is vexed, from a captain's point of view, with islands almost beyond endurance.

What can one say about the plain of Pagan, which sneaks into view on the east bank of the river, with only a few old pagodas and stupas to hint at what lies just out of sight? One of the major guidebook series, one I've frequently found outdated, monotonic, or otherwise unhelpful, states that Pagan is similar to what Europe might be like if all its medieval cathedrals had been built in one spot and then suddenly abandoned. Well, certainly the almost fanatical level of devotion was about the same.

A millennium ago Pagan was a small market town, which it has again become. In 1057 Anawratha, who used Theravada Buddhism to unify the Burmese empire for the first time, chose it as his capital. For the next two hundred and thirty years, ten other kings kept adding to the architectural wonders built by Anawratha—the walled and moated palace and the temple enclosures almost beyond enumeration. At its peak Pagan is thought to have contained thirteen thousand monuments of assorted sizes and functions. Today twenty-two hundred remain standing after various earthquakes (the most recent in 1975) and assorted man-made disasters. Many others are heaps of bricks and rubble now impossible to imagine as part of the golden-spired city, where Burmese came into existence as a written language and where art, commerce, and statecraft all flourished. The site is dry (cacti grow throughout the country's central plain) and perfectly flat.

Central Pagan is one of the world's major religious sites, on a par with Angkor Wat perhaps but begging for comparison with Ayutthaya, eighty-five kilometres north of Bangkok and one of Thailand's, and Asia's, most visited and venerated places. Ayutthaya was founded about 1350 and was a great imperial capital through four hundred years and fifty-three reigns (the reigns were brief in those days), the seat of the Sukhotthai kingdom that spread from Angkor in modern Cambodia to Pegu (now Bagu) in modern Burma. At its height in the seventeenth century Ayutthaya had two thousand golden spires and a population of a million, putting it on a par with London or Paris. The comparison is significant, for Ayutthaya was a truly cosmopolitan place, with Dutch and Portuguese quarters and trade extending deep into China and the Middle East. This was essentially different from Pagan, whose heart was always spiritual.

Their fates make an interesting contrast as well. Ayutthaya's great enemy was the Burmese. As I was going there once up the Chao Phraya from Bang City, the Big Chili, a guide was pointing out the unending battle between snakes and rats in the rice paddies. "They live against each other's destiny," he said with unintentional eloquence. So too the Thais and the Burmese always have done. In 1592 the two agreed to decide the fate of Ayutthaya by champions. Naresuam, the Ayutthayan king, would mount an elephant and ride out alone with a long-handled sword to meet the Burmese commander, a crown prince, equally alone and similarly equipped. Naresuam beheaded his enemy. Wat Yai Chay a Mongkol (roughly the Great Temple of Auspicious Victory) was erected to commemorate the event. It is now one of the principal sites of what is left of Ayutthaya. But the Burmese persisted century after century. Ayutthaya was well defended, a site built on three rivers with a canal cut across the fourth side to make a huge island fortress. Finally, in 1767, the Burmese broke through and sacked and burned it, killing or enslaving most of the inhabitants. Ayutthaya never grew back.

Pagan's fate was different in important ways. The city survived long enough to undergo a natural period of decline, even decadence. Its last king, Narathinhapate, drove the community towards bankruptcy by a genuinely obsessive and ostentatious programme of temple-building to earn ever more merit, as all the while Kublai Khan's army, having subdued southern China, made menacing movements. Rather than pay Khan tribute, Narathinhapate began razing stupas in order to build more fortifications. But instead of allowing himself to be besieged, Narathinhapate moved north in 1287 with thirty thousand troops and engaged a force of ten thousand Mogul archers on what is now the Burmese-Chinese border. He was defeated soundly. Khan occupied Pagan but didn't destroy it. Eventually the Moguls withdrew and Pagan was allowed to crumble. To the outside world it didn't hold much interest until Victorian times, just as Angkor was "discovered" a short while later. Such at least is the most commonly accepted version of Pagan's destiny. A recent trend in Burmese historiography is to downplay racial conflict between the ethnic Burmans and the Moguls and to emphasize political, social, and economic inevitabilities. In any event, there I was at Pagan.

My preference would have been a saddle horse, but there was none to be seen. Pagan does have many pony carts for hire, however, and I hauled my body into one of these and asked to be taken to Shwezigon Pagoda, the enormous golden temple built by Anawratha to commemorate the successful transplantation of Theravada Buddhism from India to Burma. It is supposed to house one of Buddha's collarbones as well as a replica of one of his teeth. The pagoda's bell shape is thought to be the original for all the subsequent ones identified with Burmese religious architecture. Then the cart was off at a trot to the opposite side of the city to Htilominlo Temple, forty-six metres high and with fascinating traces of ancient murals and plasterwork. While many temples may retain their old gold or have had more reapplied, the characteristic look of Pagan is reddish brick and slightly lighter sandstone. From the top of one temple—I had to crawl ascending narrow stairs, using a borrowed torch; the effort almost did me in—I could look from all points of the compass and see monuments, in sizes from small chedis to small palaces, sitting pell-mell on the parched landscape.

"In those days people build temple," my horseman said in broken English. "Today's people build hotel. Joint ventures."

He looked as though he were about to spit in contempt. His point was well made. Pagan today is at least as much about tourism as it is about meditation, if not a great deal more so. But people, including overseas Chinese and other foreigners, continue to earn merit by paying for the reconstruction of various monuments, deeds which are then recorded on plaques near by. This not only eases the financial strain on the drug-rich government, which needs cash for keeping down the people, but also gives parts of Pagan the feel of one of those wealthy American universities where every tree seems to bear the name of a wealthy alum.

Beyond that the driver didn't say much, despite my attempts to draw him out on the subject of horses, a tactic I find usually works at least as well as baby pictures. He was clearly alarmed, however, when I asked him to stop so I could snap a picture of the National League for Democracy in Pagan village: a small office behind an aquamarine wall beneath a large, defiantly red sign in both Burmese and English. Believe me, I was surprised to see so obvious an arm of Suu Kyi's party permitted such prominence in the heart of the modest township, close to the lovely street market and the typically British traffic roundabout. I was sure it wouldn't be so in Mandalay. Driver and horse both seemed relieved when my shutter clicked and we passed on, headed for the jetty at Ngaung U, where I was to board my connecting boat.

This shorter leg of the journey was a much more pleasant experience, partly because I travelled on a much better class of vessel, with air con, a comfortable cabin, and decent food. Since the still rigidly controlled tourism business started, the government has allowed out-side entrepreneurs to operate either luxury- or expedition-style boats on the river. Most are German-built vessels formerly used on the Rhine. Such is the case with the top-of-the-line boat operated by the revived Orient Express group, which has branched out from fancy train routes, including one from Singapore to Bangkok and Chiang Mai. So too with a different British firm, which bought the rights to the name Irrawaddy Flotilla and was running another European passenger boat, built for about two hundred people. Someone, I was told, has even raised one of the hulks of the original Flotilla and refitted it.

North of Pagan, the river was even more enormously wide and the shadowy mountains stood like chaperons in the distance on either side of the valley. Again there were many islands. How many would be visible in the rainy season I couldn't say, but some were so big they seemed to be the opposite bank of the river. This produced an eerie effect, one bank (sometimes port, sometimes starboard) being comparatively lush and green while the other looked like a scene on the Arabian peninsula. At times it was almost as though we were chugging up the Nile, not the Irrawaddy; I wouldn't have been surprised if a dhow had passed us, going in the opposite direction. What did pass us, or we them, was a strange assortment of com-mercial craft, including tugs pushing coal barges three abreast, miniature freighters and, to my surprise, a small tanker. To my sur-prise because I thought a tanker of any size would have drawn too much water, which was why liquids were nosed upstream on fuel barges or else transported in drums. There were general cargo-and-passenger boats of all description, some of pilot-house construction, others homemade-looking and bare, at least one with the upswept stern and aft superstructure that reminded me of the wrecked East Indiaman I had seen in the Falklands. But then this territory was and is Indochina indeed. The fact that the British ended up with it rather than the French blinds the West to this view, which seems so obvious when one is actually in Burma, where even the cuisine is naturally enough a singular compound of Indian and Chinese.

The higher the banks, the greater the evidence of the erosion caused by flooding. In some places several different strata of subsoil were exposed, with a layer of limestone here, a parallel one of red clay there, showing how the river gives and takes away, rearranging the land each year as though it were shuffling a deck of cards. The dwellings clustered into little brown hamlets were built on stilts, of course, but not with the same hope of relative permanence as stilt houses elsewhere. The two sides of a house most vulnerable to the monsoon are the most strongly made, using sheets of split bamboo that look like vertical venetian blinds. People simply assume that these and the roof will need replacing every two or three years. Yet sometimes they are too optimistic, and entire villages have the soil stripped out from under them and have to be rebuilt on higher ground, which in time will prove to be right on the water's edge again. It's not unknown for fairly large stupas to tumble into the river and be swept away. But now, early in the year, all was peaceful, relaxing. Crops that do well in alluvial soil were certainly healthy-looking. The corn was high. Each village had a well-worn path to the place where the men's fishing boats were beached at night. Women trudged along these narrow walkways with baskets and even large clay pots on their heads, maintaining perfect balance without using their hands: a common sight all over Asia but a fact that never fails to amaze me, like some magic trick one has seen performed repeatedly but can't quite figure out.

The first *ma* or town after Bagan is Pookku, traditionally a seat of both boat-building and monasticism. Another twenty-five kilometres or so and one comes to the place where the Irrawaddy is greeted by its main tributary, the Chindwin, flowing down from the far north-west. The partnership of the two produced an enormous island, perhaps fifty kilometres long by seven or eight wide. The back or western channel isn't navigable by big boats, so we took the main or Myinguan channel, passing such places as Yandabo and Sameikkon. At the former the Burmese signed the treaty of capitulation at the end of the First Anglo-Burmese War in 1826, while the latter, being full of old colonial homes and warehouses, shows what happened as a result. Above Sameikkon, before the island ends and the watercourse turns due east, is an enormous white-domed temple, the Kaunjadaw Pagoda, erected by King Thalun the year before his faraway fellow monarch, Queen Victoria, ascended the throne. Size is what distinguishes it from the many others, for at one point on the upper stretch of the river I counted the tops of forty temples in view at one time. This was near Sagaing, another of the ancient capitals, which lays claim to being the spiritual headquarters of this most spiritual of nations. Sagaing is also where you can see the Ava Bridge, which doesn't actually run to the town of that name, the only place in Burma to have been the capital on two different occasions, for Ava is located on an island that can be reached only by boat. The Ava Bridge is a ten-hump railway span built in 1934 by the British, who partly destroyed it during the Japanese occupation, then rebuilt it just at the time of Independence in 1948. It remains, though not for much longer, the only bridge across the Irrawaddy.

After you pass under the bridge, the river makes a sharp turn due north. Mandalay isn't far distant now, a matter of a couple of hours, but the river is still wild, strange, and sometimes unpredictable— both in the way certain familiar views repeat themselves randomly and through the addition of relatively new sights. Here people draw their water from concrete wells using buckets on ropes; even though the river is only a few metres away, this is how they prefer to bathe, though many still drink from the river, buying water treated with alum from roving tank trunks. The channel here is so full of switch-backs that sometimes we weren't more than a few metres from shore, close enough at one point for us to reach out over the rail and touch the roots of a tree stump ripped out of the ground by the last flood. The wildlife as well seemed to announce that change was imminent.

Once the bank was lined with thousands of crows, vast crowds of them waiting by the water's edge as though expecting some crow-ferry to pick them up and deposit them on the opposite side. At other times the sky was full of a fast bright yellow bird I had never seen before. And then there we were at the public landing in Mandalay. Lines were being prepared and people on shore were making ready to receive them. One of our crew pulled the rope on the ship's bell to signal the engineer and the world of our arrival.

I was ambivalent about Mandalay, after the tense bustle of the much larger Rangoon. Mine isn't the usual reaction of the Burmese themselves, certainly not that of Mandalay's residents, who claim to speak purer Burmese and be more cultured generally than their counterparts from other places. Yes, there is a splendid royal palace, for this was the final capital of precolonial Burma before the British captured it, and the site of a once-mighty fortress, now once again occupied by the military. And, of course, there are Buddhist sites in limitless abundance. But I found the sense of superiority insupportable. Generally speaking, the farther north one goes in Burma, the less one sees of oxen and buffalo and the more one sees of horses. Here the general principle of increasing civilization is turned in on itself. Here there are pony carts in the poorer areas and enclosed carriages in the others.

No one can deny that this is the heart of the country's agriculture and also of most of the craft industries, both its rice bowl and its centre of gold-beating, weaving, and embroidery. Numerous earthquakes, however, have done considerable damage and so, of course, has the central government which, for example, razed the old market and hopes to relocate the people who live on the waterfront and give it its character. Once you're outside the tight central core, Mandalay suffers even more in comparison to Rangoon. The streets are narrower, the parks new and nasty, the people poorer. I don't mean that it is necessarily inferior to Rangoon. In some ways life seems better: the military is much less conspicuous in the streets of

Mandalay than in the present capital.

M had given me the name of someone in Mandalay to contact. I discovered there is a single telephone directory for the entire country of fifty million. Taking white pages and yellow pages together, it is about the thickness of a North American phone book for a community of perhaps one hundred and fifty thousand or two hundred thousand people. That's a measure of the organic poverty as well as of the deliberate policy of poverty. When I located the friend, and we arranged a meeting, he showed me some of the points of interest. It was the time of day when school let out and the streets were full of girls in blue-and-white uniforms.

"Since the system of government schools, all pupils now begin to study English in Grade One," he said.

"Are there private schools as well?" I asked.

"Yes, but these teach no Burmese language or Burmese culture. They are for the children of the high military, rich businessmen, people in drugs."

His own English was almost as fluent as M's, but without the same musicality or the British vowels, and he would sometimes stub his toe on an idiom. A certain monastery, he pointed out, "possesses eight hundred of monks." This suddenly reminded me of my long-dead Welsh grandfather, who would use phrases such as "a thousand of ten-penny nails."

Like the colonialists of old, we considered seeking relief from the heat by leaving the city. Not far away there is actually an old British hill station, Pyin Oo Lwin, designed for this very purpose. I suggested an even higher elevation much farther afield: the small city of Magok, about two hundred kilometres north, the world's most important source of rubies, particularly the coveted pigeon-blood ones. Near Inya Lake in Rangoon I had seen the building where the junta holds its annual wholesale gem fair, inviting a select number of jewellery manufacturers from round the world, much as De Beers does in South Africa with its diamonds. Under the junta's monopoly, production at the mines, still worked by hand, has fallen off. This has caused Rangoon to double the frequency of the fair and also to open a scaled-down retail version for individuals. This decision has probably contributed to the problem, endemic throughout Burma and Thailand, of dealers selling fake rubies and other gems to gullible tourists, a situation that keeps the highly efficient Thai Tourist Police quite busy. The problem is compounded by the fact that rubies can now be manufactured using alum heated to extreme temperatures. These are genuine rubies as much as industrial diamonds are genuine diamonds, and yet they aren't repositories of wealth. Rather, they are simply proof that the alchemists of old were closer to the truth of transmutation than we believe they were; their stumbling block was their innocent idea that scientific breakthroughs would come to those who are decent and purest of heart rather than to those who are the most skilled technologists.

"I fear that Magok is once again off-limits to foreigners," my companion said in a low voice. "It used to be accessible by special permit, but no longer."

I thought: *Oh no, not more sneaking round the rules and regulations. This one's probably an informer too.*

"Maybe we can at least set off in that direction," I said. "Doesn't it stand to reason that the closer one gets to Magok, the easier it will be to buy real stones instead of fakes?"

"One would think so," he said. But I sensed dubiety in his voice. "Indeed, this is so. But not for the reason you might suppose."

I asked him what he meant.

He was speaking very softly again. "Unscrupulous men have the same idea as yourself. Thinking that people will believe that their rubies are genuine because they were bought in Magok, they go there to sell their fakes." Now his voice was like a mouse's whisper. "I do not know this as a personal fact, but I am told that when one of these men is caught in the area he is—I have sometimes been told this—killed. Shot on the spot, I believe you say, with bullet to the head. In this way the good name of Magok is preserved."

"By the government?"

He smiled wanly but said nothing except to repeat that we couldn't go there.

In a few days I was back in Bangkok, once more in the middle of a security crackdown. This time there was one VIP to protect, the prime minister of what appeared to be the slowly disintegrating Indonesian federation. The usual suspects were assisting police with their preparations. I was becoming sick of politics.

On the long trip to Vancouver by way of Hong Kong (my first time there since the Handover), I kept thinking of M and how I would miss her and how little I trusted her and how we might find some way of keeping in touch when each of us was out-of-bounds to the other. Maybe, I thought, that is the way of reconciling the conflicting emotions. I was, as usual, being a fool.

Another letter from M reached me in Vancouver, then another, then many more. They didn't discuss politics as we had done during our strolls round Rangoon. Nor did they hint at the infatuation that had been the subject of the confession she slipped under my door that night. Instead, they dealt matter-of-factly with her intention of visiting me in Canada; she sometimes mentioned the bureaucracy she was forced to deal with in getting the Directorate of Defence Services Intelligence to return her passport. So saying, though, she got it back in what I thought must surely be record time—at what price I could only guess. She also appeared to come into money rather suddenly, enough to go overseas for a while. She wasn't proposing to travel on the cheap as I had done, but would fly to Bangkok and then directly to Vancouver. All this represented an enormous outlay for someone whose circumstances I thought I knew. It was also, of course, an extraordinary move for someone who professed never to have ventured outside her own country.

I didn't discourage her from visiting, partly because I sensed that persuasion was futile but primarily because I was curious as to what might happen. Was she in the pay of Kin Nyunt, Burma's despised intelligence chief? I couldn't quite convince myself that this was likely. For one thing, she didn't appear slick enough, but then I didn't know how slick such people aspired to be. In any case, the reasons she gave for her actions, indeed the actions themselves, struck me as highly implausible. My guess is that the DDSI encourages translators and others who have business with visiting foreigners to develop friendships with them, with the object of learning their intentions—whether, for example, they're writers, whom the government so fears. Or maybe she approached them with a plan. Who knows? I was curious to see her design unfold so I might determine her motives. In that sense, I guess, we were both acting like the spooks that temperament has not cut us out to be.

She stayed for nearly two weeks while she and I did our respective dances round each other's lives. For example, she seemed quite interested in the shelf of books about Burma that I had in my office. I was unable to determine, however, whether they interested her as proof of my hostile intentions or merely because they were banned at home. Similarly I couldn't accurately judge her interest, admittedly rather casual, in Burmese exile groups and human-rights organizations in Canada. What disturbed me from the first was the way she reversed her previous opinions on the events in Burma. A genuine democrat could be forgiven for not talking politics inside the country but loosening up once outside. M was the reverse. In Rangoon she had shown me her admiration for the Lady and her contempt for the military drug dealers; now, in Canada, she was defending the regime or, rather, attacking its critics.

Needless to say, we didn't have a love affair. There was, however, one moment that touched me deeply. As a polite host, and moreover one who wanted to keep an eye on her without being too blatant, I took her on a great many sight-seeing excursions: Stanley Park, the Granville Island market, Chinatown—all the usual. She was impressed by Stanley Park with its unfamiliar plant life but didn't quite see the point of going to the market or Chinatown as both of them looked like clean versions of what she was familiar with back home. One day we were downtown, walking south on Howe Street, opposite the Four Seasons. She was craning her neck, looking up at the tall buildings.

"All of these structures made of large glass squares," she said. "Can you tell me, please, how they keep them clean? Do they shoot up soapy water with powerful fire hoses, or do they climb upon bamboo scaffolds with cotton cloth?"

Suddenly remembering all the ridiculous questions I'd put to patient hosts in other parts of the world, I replied I couldn't be certain, but I thought their method was closer to the second than to the first.

After a week and a half, we'd worn each other out, and neither of us, I suspect, had reached any definite conclusions about the other. Thereupon she suddenly announced she was going to England to stay with another acquaintance for whom she had once translated and with whom she had kept in touch.

"That's a very expensive flight from here," I said. "Halfway round the world."

"Oh, I already have the ticket," she told me.

And off she went; I never heard from her again.

Aung San Suu Kyi had been under house arrest in Rangoon for nineteen months when, in May 2002, her most recent period of confinement ended. After more than a year's speculation, she was released and allowed to travel within the city and indeed throughout the country. What this showed most clearly perhaps was not that her long protest was paying off at last but that the junta was finally getting clever about spin. Within days the *New York Times* ran a travel piece debating whether it would now be politically correct for Americans to journey to Burma and spend freely. Days after that the actor Angelina Jolie visited Burmese refugees in Thailand, no doubt the first of many Hollywood celebrities to do so in the rush to find the next Tibet and the new Dalai Lama.

Does Suu Kyi's release signal fundamental change for the better? I'm sceptical but admit that no one knows. Suu Kyi herself has been careful not to get people's hopes up. She knows the regime was badly frightened by the attempted countercoup by the family of Ne Win, the nonagenarian who overthrew Burmese democracy in 1962, thus starting the present nightmare. And all observers see how the military's greed and mismanagement, combined perhaps, I admit, with the economic sanctions of the West, have brought so much chaos to the economy that the customary electrical brownouts have become blackouts. The economy in fact is in a shambles. The country continues to do well in natural-resource exports: teak and gems. What with the American war in Afghanistan, it has even gained market share with value-added agricultural products: heroin. But Burma's main exportable manufactured goods are barbed wire and methamphetamines. And the barbed wire is only what's surplus to the needs of the domestic market, which uses the stuff by the kilometre to imprison dissenters, democrats, and ethnic minorities.